HOLD

THE SUFFERING ECONOMY OF CUSTOMER SERVICE

And the Revolt That's Long Overdue

AMAS TENUMAH

DEDICATION

For my mother Christie, my father William, and my brother Bobby

Whose memories inspire me every day.

PART I

THE BROKEN PROMISE

How the social contract of customer service was betrayed for profit

CHAPTER 1

THE 4,000-YEAR COMPLAINT

Section 1: The Eternal Complaint

Tell Ea-nasir: Nanni sends the following message in 1750 BC:

> *When you came, you said to me as follows: "I will give Gimil-Sin (when he comes) fine quality copper ingots." You left then but you did not do what you promised me. You put ingots which were not good before my messenger (Sit-Sin) and said: "If you want to take them, take them; if you do not want to take them, go away!"*

What do you take me for, that you treat somebody like me with such contempt? I have sent as messengers gentlemen like ourselves to collect the bag with my money (deposited with you) but you have treated me with contempt by sending them back to me empty-handed several times, and that through enemy territory. Is there anyone among the merchants who trade with Telmun who has treated me in this way? You alone treat my messenger with contempt! On account of that one (trifling) mina of silver which I owe(?) you, you feel free to speak in such a way, while I have given to the palace on your behalf 1,080 pounds of copper, and umi-abum has likewise given 1,080 pounds of copper, apart from what we both have had written on a sealed tablet to be kept in the temple of Samas.

How have you treated me for that copper? You have withheld my money bag from me in enemy territory; it is now up to you to restore (my money) to me in full.

Take cognizance that (from now on) I will not accept here any copper from you that is not of fine quality. I shall (from now on) select and take the ingots individually in my own yard, and I shall exercise against you my right of rejection because you have treated me with contempt.

The words above were written over 4,000 years ago. They sound like a customer service email written 40 minutes ago.

In four millennia, we've invented the internet, put computers in our pockets, and landed robots on Mars. But somehow, customer service has barely evolved past cuneiform tablets and righteous indignation.

If anything, it's gotten worse.

From Ea-nasir to Customer Service Hell

Nanni's complaint has everything: broken promises, poor quality products, rude treatment, runaround between departments, having to deal with middlemen instead of decision-makers, payment disputes, and threats to take his business elsewhere.

Sound familiar?

But here's what Nanni had that you don't: Ea-nasir was a real person he could track down and yell at. Ea-nasir lived in the same city. They probably knew each other. If Ea-nasir's business practices were systematically terrible, word would spread through the marketplace and he'd be finished.

Nanni had leverage.

Today, your complaint gets routed through chatbots, outsourced call centers, and policy labyrinths designed by people you'll never meet, working for companies that profit from your frustration.

The merchant you're angry at might be a faceless corporation with no physical presence in your city, your state, or even your country. The person handling your complaint has no authority to fix your problem and no personal stake in whether you're satisfied.

The CEO who created the policies that caused your problem will never hear about your experience. The shareholders who profit from cost-cutting customer service will never know your name.

The 4,000-Year-Round Trip

Customer service has completed a perfect round trip back to systematic indifference.

Ea-nasir treated customers with contempt because he could get away with it in the short term. Modern companies treat customers with contempt because they can get away with it in the short term.

The difference is scale.

Ea-nasir could rip off maybe a few dozen customers before his reputation caught up with him. Modern companies can systematically frustrate millions of customers while their stock price goes up and their executives get bonuses for "operational efficiency."

Nanni carved his complaint into clay and hand-delivered it. You fill out web forms that disappear into digital void, navigate phone trees designed to exhaust you, and chat with bots programmed to deflect rather than resolve.

Nanni expected Ea-nasir to read his complaint personally. You hope someone, somewhere, might eventually see your feedback after it's been filtered through multiple systems and reduced to a satisfaction score.

Nanni threatened to take his business elsewhere and actually could. You threaten to take your business elsewhere and discover that all of Ea-nasir's competitors have the same terrible customer service because they all use the same cost-cutting playbook.

The Technology Trap

The cruelest irony is that we have technology Nanni could never have imagined, and we use it to make customer service worse, not better.

We can track packages in real-time as they cross continents, but we can't get straight answers about why your order was canceled.

We have AI that can write poetry and solve complex mathematical equations, but chatbots that can't understand "I want to cancel my subscription."

We can book flights, hotels, and rental cars in minutes, but it takes hours to fix a simple billing error.

Every innovation that should have made customer service better was hijacked to make it cheaper instead. Every tool that could have enhanced human connection was deployed to avoid human contact.

The Permanent Present

The most disturbing thing about Nanni's complaint isn't how old it is, it's how current it feels.

Change a few details and this could be your experience with any company this week:

Tell Amazon: I ordered fine quality headphones. You left then but you did not do what you promised me. You put headphones which were not good before my doorstep and when I tried to return them, your chatbot said: "If you want to keep them, keep them; if you do not want to keep them, go to our website!"

What do you take me for, that you treat somebody like me with such contempt? I have sent messages gentlemen like me (through your chat system) but you have treated me with contempt by sending them back to me with form responses several times, and that through your phone tree maze. Is there anyone among the retailers who trade online who has treated me in this way? You alone treat my messenger with contempt!

Take cognizance that (from now on) I will not accept here any products from you that are not of fine quality. I shall (from now on) select and take my business individually to your competitors, and I shall exercise against you my right of rejection because you have treated me with contempt.

The template is identical. Only technology has changed.

The Sophistication Paradox

We've gotten incredibly sophisticated at being terrible to customers.

Ea-nasir's rudeness was personal and direct. Modern customer service rudeness is systematized and optimized. It's been A/B tested, cost analyzed and refined across millions of interactions.

Companies have spent billions of dollars and decades of research to perfect the art of:

Making you wait just long enough to be frustrated but not long enough to give up

Sounding helpful while providing no actual help

Creating enough steps in every process to tire you out

Designing policies that sound reasonable but are impossible to navigate

Training representatives to apologize profusely while being completely powerless

Ancient merchants were bad at customer service by accident or personal character flaws. Modern companies are bad at customer service by design and deliberate strategy.

The Universal Experience

What makes Nanni's complaint so powerful isn't just its age, it's its universality.

Every culture, every economic system, every era has produced some version of this complaint. The merchant who promises quality and delivers garbage. The business that takes your money and then treats you with contempt. The system that protects sellers at the expense of buyers.

But for most of human history, these were exceptions that proved the rule. Bad merchants went out of business. Word of mouth punished companies that mistreated customers. Market forces created natural consequences for poor service.

Today, bad customer service is the rule. Good customer service is the exception that surprises us so much we post about it on social media.

We've built an economic system where Ea-nasir's behavior isn't just tolerated, it's rewarded. Companies that treat customers with systematic contempt report record profits. Executives who cut customer service costs get promoted. Shareholders who profit from customer misery never face consequences.

The Eternal Truth

Nanni's complaint reveals an eternal truth about commerce: the relationship between buyer and seller contains inherent tension.

The seller wants to maximize profit while minimizing effort and accountability. The buyer wants to maximize value while minimizing risk and frustration.

For thousands of years, market forces kept this tension in balance. Sellers who pushed too hard toward their own interests at the expense of buyers would lose customers and fail.

But something fundamental has changed in the modern economy. The market forces that once protected customers have been neutralized by scale, technology, and financial engineering.

Companies can now treat customers terribly and thrive. The natural consequences that once punished bad service have been eliminated or delayed so far into the future that they don't affect quarterly earnings.

Nanni lived in a world where customer service had to work because the alternative was business failure. We live in a world where customer service doesn't have to work because the alternative is... slightly lower profit margins.

The Question That Haunts Us

If Nanni's complaint from 1750 BC reads like a modern customer service experience, what does that say about progress?

What does it say about civilization that we've advanced in every other area of human endeavor: medicine, communication, transportation, science but gone backward in the simple act of treating customers with dignity?

What does it say about our economic system that it can produce miraculous innovations while simultaneously creating customer service experiences that would have been familiar to ancient Mesopotamians?

Technology has changed. The sophistication has increased. The scale has exploded.

But the fundamental disrespect for customers, the casual contempt, the broken promises, the bureaucratic runaround remains exactly the same.

The Promise of This Book

Nanni's complaint survived 4,000 years because someone thought it was important enough to preserve. Someone recognized that this wasn't just one angry customer, it was evidence of a system that had broken down.

Today, millions of people have experiences just like Nanni's every day. But instead of carving them into clay tablets for posterity, we vent on social media, hang up in frustration, or just accept that terrible customer service is the price of modern life.

This book is the clay tablet for our era.

It's the record of how we got from personal accountability to systematized indifference. It's the evidence of a system that has broken down not by accident, but by design.

But unlike Nanni, we don't have to just complain and hope for the best. We can understand why the system works this way, who benefits from it, and how to change it.

We can trace the path from Ea-nasir's marketplace contempt to modern corporate contempt. We can identify the economic forces that reward bad service and the technological innovations that enable it at scale.

Most importantly, we can chart a path back to customer service that actually serves customers.

The social contract wasn't always broken. For most of human history, customer service worked because the incentives were aligned. To understand how we lost that alignment and how to get it back we need to go back to the beginning.

We need to see how customer service evolved from personal accountability to corporate avoidance, one broken promise at a time.

Section 2: The Broken Promise

Nanni's complaint from 1750 BC reveals something profound: customer service was built on a social contract that worked for thousands of years until recently.

Let me state that social contract plainly:

When you buy a product or service, you're not just buying that product or service. You're also quietly buying an insurance policy with a promise that if something goes wrong, a human being somewhere will pick up the phone, solve your problem, and maybe even sound like they give a damn.

That's the unspoken agreement of commerce. Customer service is the claims department.

The Insurance You Didn't Know You Bought

Most people still think of customer service as a "nice to have" a bonus feature, like heated seats or an extended warranty. But it's not.

Customer service is the payout mechanism. It's how companies deliver on the rest of the value proposition they dangled in front of you. When something breaks, ships late, misfires, or just doesn't work like it should, you're filing a claim on the policy you prepaid with your purchase.

Think about it: every transaction contains an implicit promise that extends far beyond the moment money changes hands.

When you buy a car, you're not just buying metal, plastic, and rubber. You're buying the promise that if the transmission fails, someone will fix it. If the airbag recalls your model, someone will contact you. If you have questions about your warranty, someone will explain it.

When you sign up for a streaming service, you're not just buying access to movies. You're buying the promise that if your account gets hacked, someone will help you recover it. If you're charged incorrectly, someone will fix the billing. If the service doesn't work, someone will troubleshoot it.

When you order something online, you're not just buying the product. You're buying the promise that if it arrives broken, someone will replace it. If it never arrives, someone will track it down. If it's not what was advertised, someone will make it right.

This insurance policy is baked into the price of everything you buy. It's not free. It's not a perk. It's part of the deal. It's what you were promised.

The Claims Department Problem

And just like insurance companies, most businesses want to make damn sure they don't pay that claim if they can help it.

Have you ever tried to cancel a subscription and ended up in a labyrinth of dark patterns, dropdown menus, and "are you sure you want to leave?" hostage negotiations? That's denial of coverage.

Have you ever sat through a chatbot loop so maddening you started doubting your own humanity? That's the digital version of a $500 deductible.

Have you ever waited 14 days for an email response that just said, "please refer to our FAQ"? That's the customer service equivalent of an insurance adjuster ghosting your calls.

I'm not being cynical. I'm just telling you the design.

Here's the math running in their heads: They already have your money. From that moment on, every interaction with you is a cost. Not an opportunity. A cost.

And when you reach out to customer service, that's a signal something didn't go right. That signal costs money to acknowledge. It costs even more to resolve. If a human gets involved? That's a catastrophic loss on their internal actuarial table.

The Deflection Doctrine

The most profitable insurance companies in the world have figured something out: if you make the claims process just annoying enough, just slow enough, just bureaucratic enough... some percentage of people will give up. They'll eat the loss. Move on.

Congratulations you just protected your margin.

The customer service playbook is identical.

Before you think I'm exaggerating, know this: most customer service teams don't measure how well they resolve problems. They measure how well they deflect them.

Deflection. Let that word settle in. It's a bureaucrat's synonym for "go away."

I've consulted for companies that celebrate 78% deflection rates. Seventy eight percent of customers who sought help never spoke to a human being. They measured this as a success metric, not a failure.

And this is where the social contract starts to fray.

The Great Expectation Gap

Because we, as customers, still believe in the deal. We still think we're owed something when things break. A little effort. A little dignity. Someone with a pulse and a clue.

We believe that if something doesn't work or the experience falls apart, we can call someone who's empowered, informed, and motivated to help.

But that's not the deal we're actually being offered anymore.

We're being sold goods and services with the assumption that customer service will be there if we need it. But behind the scenes, the incentives are clear: shrink the safety net, hide it behind a chatbot, bury it under a 48-hour autoresponder.

The promise is still being made. But the delivery mechanism has been systematically dismantled.

The Accountability Vacuum

In Nanni's time, accountability was personal and immediate. If Ea-nasir delivered bad copper, Nanni knew exactly who to blame and how to find them.

Today, accountability has been distributed across so many layers of corporate structure that it's essentially disappeared.

Your problem with Amazon isn't really Amazon's fault, it's the fault of the third-party seller. Your problem with the third-party seller isn't their fault it's the fault of their supplier. Your problem with the supplier isn't their fault it's the fault of shipping logistics. Your problem with shipping logistics isn't their fault it's the fault of weather/traffic/union strikes/global supply chain disruptions.

Everyone is sorry. Nobody is responsible.

The customer service representative you finally reach after 45 minutes on hold has no connection to the people who made the product, set the policies, designed the website, or decided to outsource customer support to reduce costs.

They're just the person unlucky enough to answer the phone when your frustration finally boiled over.

The Promise vs. Reality Matrix

Here's what companies promise in their marketing versus what they deliver in their customer service:

Promise: "Your satisfaction is our top priority"

Reality: Your satisfaction is measured quarterly and optimized for cost, not outcome

Promise: "We're here for you 24/7"

Reality: We're here to deflect you 24/7 through automated systems designed to exhaust you

Promise: "Customer service is our passion"

Reality: Customer service is our cost center, and costs must be minimized

Promise: "We value your feedback"

Reality: We value your feedback when it's positive and can be used for marketing; negative feedback gets routed to satisfaction surveys designed to generate favorable scores

Promise: "We stand behind our products"

Reality: We stand behind our products with a wall of policies, procedures, and representatives with no authority to actually stand behind anything

The promises are made by marketing departments trying to differentiate from competitors. The reality is delivered by operations departments trying to hit cost targets.

The Emotional Betrayal

What makes modern customer service, so infuriating isn't just that it's inefficient, it's that it feels like emotional betrayal.

You were sold a relationship ("We care about you!") and delivered a transaction ("Press 1 for billing").

You were promised partnership ("We're on your side!") and given adversarial negotiations ("I can't do that, but I can offer you 10% off your next purchase").

You were sold empathy ("We understand your frustration") and delivered scripts written by legal departments to minimize liability.

The gap between promise and delivery creates something worse than mere dissatisfaction. It creates the feeling of being lied to. Of being taken advantage of. Of being treated with contempt.

That's why customer service interactions feel so personal even when the problems are obviously systemic. You're not just angry about the broken product or billing error. You're angry about the broken promise.

The Default Excuse

Every company has learned to blame customer service failures on "higher than expected volume."

"We're experiencing higher than expected call volumes. Your estimated wait time is... 47 minutes."

Higher than expected? Really? You've been in business for 20 years and you still can't predict that people might call for help?

Or here's a thought: maybe the volume isn't higher than expected. Maybe you just staffed for the volume you wanted rather than the volume you knew you'd get.

"Due to COVID-19, we're experiencing higher than normal call volumes."

That message is still playing in 2025, five years after the pandemic ended. COVID became the permanent excuse for temporary service degradation.

The Optimization Trap

Companies have optimized customer service for everything except customer satisfaction.

They've optimized for:

Cost per contact (make each interaction as cheap as possible)

Average handle time (get customers off the phone as quickly as possible)

Deflection rate (prevent customers from reaching humans)

Automation rate (replace humans with machines wherever possible)

Containment rate (prevent escalations to supervisors)

Notice what's missing from that list? Anything about whether customers actually get their problems solved.

The optimization has become so sophisticated that companies can show improving metrics in every category while customer satisfaction plummets.

"Our call center efficiency is up 23%!" (Because customers give up before reaching anyone)

"Our automation rate increased 40%!" (Because humans are harder to reach)

"Our cost per contact dropped 15%!" (Because the contacts that do happen provide less human help)

The Warranty Illusion

Extended warranties are the perfect example of the broken promise in action.

Companies sell you additional "protection" and "peace of mind," then make claiming that protection so difficult that most people never use it.

I've analyzed warranty claim data for major retailers. Here's the typical pattern:

Extended warranties sold: 340,000 annually

Warranty claims filed: 12% (40,800)

Claims actually honored: 67% of those filed (27,336)

Total customers who successfully used their warranty: 8% of those who bought it

Eight percent. You bought insurance from a company, then that same company made it so hard to use the insurance that 92% of customers never successfully claimed it.

That's not customer service. That's fraud with a customer service department attached.

The Social Media False Hope

For a brief moment, social media seemed like it might fix the accountability problem. Companies couldn't hide behind call centers and ticket systems when complaints were public.

But they learned to game that system too.

Now you get responses like: "We're sorry to hear about your experience! Please DM us your account details so we can look into this privately."

Translation: "We'll acknowledge your complaint publicly, so other people see us responding, then handle it privately using the same broken system that failed you in the first place."

Social media customer service became a theater. The performance of caring without the substance of helping.

The Breaking Point

The social contract is breaking down because one side stopped honoring it while continuing to collect payment for it.

Companies take your money with promises of support, then deliver systems designed to avoid providing that support. They sell you insurance policies they have no intention of honoring. They promise relationships they have no intention of maintaining.

And they act surprised when customers get angry.

But here's what they've miscalculated: the cost of broken promises compounds over time.

Every customer who gets run through the deflection gauntlet tells other people about it. Every person who gets transferred six times and still doesn't get help becomes an anti advocate for your brand. Every human being who gets treated with systematic contempt remembers that treatment long after they've solved their problem through other means.

The short-term cost savings from bad customer service create long term damage that doesn't show up in quarterly reports but shows up in market share, brand reputation, and customer lifetime value (how much a customer spends over time).

The Promise We Need

Now, to be fair some companies still honor the social contract. You know them when you find them. They feel like a warm blanket after a cold shower. You hang up the phone and say, "Wow. That was... surprisingly good."

That shouldn't be rare. But it is.

Why? Because keeping that promise costs money today and most companies are obsessed with this quarter's margins rather than next decade's relationships.

So, they get clever. They overinvest in acquisition marketing that makes promises, and under invest in customer service that keeps them. They build machines that shout louder than their support teams can whisper. They treat customer service like a necessary evil rather than a competitive differentiator.

Every time a company cuts corners on service, they're not just saving money. They're breaking the social contract. They're defaulting on the insurance policy they made you buy.

And customers are starting to notice.

The question is: what happens when enough customers stop believing the promises? What happens when the social contract breaks down completely?

We're about to find out. Because we're living through the largest crisis of trust between companies and customers in modern history.

The promises are still being made. But fewer and fewer people believe them.

And that's where this story really begins with the recognition that customer service isn't broken by accident. It's been systematically dismantled by companies that discovered they could keep customers' money without honoring the promises that money was supposed to buy.

But to understand how we got here, we need to go back to when those promises meant something. When customer service was personal, immediate, and effective not because companies were more moral, but because they had no choice.

We need to understand how customer service worked for thousands of years before we broke it in just a few decades.

Section 3: The Universal Pain

I f I asked you to name five companies whose customer service brings you joy, you would struggle.

Go ahead. Try it. Five companies that you actually look forward to calling when you have a problem. Five brands where you think, "Thank goodness I get to deal with their customer service today."

You're probably still thinking.

That's not because you're particularly hard to please or unusually unlucky with service experiences. It's because customer service is universally painful.

To be sure, there are degrees of pain. The Department of Motor Vehicles may seem worse than a hotel chain. Spirit Airlines may feel more punishing than your local coffee shop. But scratch beneath the surface, and you'll find that all customer service is broken in its own special way.

The Tolstoy Principle

Leo Tolstoy wrote, "Happy families are all alike; every unhappy family is unhappy in its own way."

Customer service follows the same principle. Good customer service experiences are remarkably similar: fast, helpful, human, effective. But customer service failures are creative in their awfulness.

Each company has found its own unique way to make you miserable:

Airlines: Make you their hostage once you're past security, then nickel and dime you for basic human dignity

Cable companies: Give you appointment windows so wide you could fit a small vacation inside them, then charge you for the privilege of waiting

Banks: Act like they're doing you a favor by holding your own money, then charge you fees for not having enough of it

Insurance companies: Take your money enthusiastically for decades, then fight every claim like you're trying to steal from them

Government agencies: Design systems so Byzantine that you need a PhD in bureaucracy just to renew your driver's license

Tech companies: Hide behind "algorithms" and "policy violations" to avoid taking responsibility for anything

It may be wait times, access to human support, lack of follow-up, impossible policies, or representatives with no authority to help. Just different flavors of pain, each expertly crafted to frustrate you in new and innovative ways.

The Great Democratization of Suffering

What's remarkable about modern customer service is how thoroughly it crosses all demographic lines.

Rich or poor, young or old, urban or rural, liberal or conservative everyone has customer service horror stories. It's one of the few shared experiences left in an increasingly divided society.

Your Republican uncle and your progressive niece may disagree about everything else, but they both hate calling their phone company. Your wealthy neighbor and your struggling colleague both dread dealing with their insurance claims. The CEO and the intern both avoid calling customer service unless absolutely necessary.

Bad customer service doesn't discriminate. It's an equal opportunity tormentor.

But here's what's even more troubling: some groups suffer disproportionately, and the companies know it.

The Accessibility Crisis

A reporter reached out to me in the winter of 2024, working on an article about how customer service fails people with disabilities. It was a topic I'm ashamed I hadn't studied deeply.

What I learned was devastating.

The bad customer service that most of us complain about is completely inaccessible to those with disabilities. We think we have it rough navigating phone trees and chatbots. For people with disabilities, these systems aren't just frustrating, they're often impossible to use.

Chatbots and online forms are inaccessible for people who can't use a mouse or have visual impairments. Screen readers can't parse most customer service websites, which are designed for visual navigation rather than accessibility.

Phone channels are a nightmare for most of us, but they're completely unusable for people with hearing disabilities. You don't even get the privilege of navigating the telephone menu from hell if you can't hear the options.

Live chat requires typing speed and reading comprehension that may not be possible for people with certain cognitive or physical disabilities.

Video chat assumes you have both audio and visual capabilities and a stable internet connection.

In-person service locations have been closing for decades, eliminating the one channel that might work best for people who struggle with technology-mediated communication.

The Americans with Disabilities Act requires equal access to services, but customer service departments routinely ignore these requirements. They build systems that work poorly for able-bodied customers and don't work at all for disabled customers.

When people with disabilities try to request accommodation, they often get routed to "specialized" departments that are even harder to reach and less empowered to help.

I spoke with a woman who needed to dispute a billing error on her phone account. She's deaf and requested TTY service. The customer service department told her to use their online chat instead. The online chat system couldn't handle her specific billing issue and told her to call the phone number. When she explained she couldn't use the phone, they suggested she have someone else call for her.

Think about that: a phone company telling a deaf customer that she needs to find someone else to make phone calls for her to resolve problems with her phone service.

This isn't just bad service, it's systematic exclusion wrapped in digital transformation rhetoric.

Companies spend millions on websites that look sleek but aren't accessible. They deploy chatbots that seem sophisticated but can't accommodate different communication needs. They eliminate human channels that worked for everyone in favor of digital channels that work only for some.

Then they act surprised when they get sued under the ADA.

The Violence Epidemic

The universal frustration with customer service has reached a breaking point that's literally dangerous.

There has been a 50% increase in violence against retail customer service workers in recent years. Think about that: customers are so frustrated with service that they're physically attacking the workers trying to help them.

The workers who get attacked aren't the executives who designed the systems that frustrate customers. They're not the consultants who recommended cost-cutting measures. They're not the shareholders who profit from understaffed customer service departments.

They're minimum-wage employees with no authority to fix the policies that create customer rage.

A Target employee gets screamed at because the website said an item was in stock but it's not on the shelf. A McDonald's worker gets threatened because the ice cream machine is broken again. An airline gate agent gets pushed because flights are oversold and delayed.

These workers didn't create the inventory systems, the equipment maintenance policies, or the overbooking algorithms that caused the problems. They're just the human faces attached to inhuman systems.

But they're the ones who absorb the anger when those systems fail.

I can't call 1-800 numbers in front of young children anymore. Not because of explicit content, but because I know I'll end up yelling "representative!" at a machine designed to ignore me.

The technology has turned customer service interactions into exercises in controlled rage. We start calm and become progressively more frustrated as we're transferred, put on hold, asked to repeat information, and given solutions that don't address our problems.

By the time we reach a human, we're already angry at the system. But the human becomes the target for that anger.

The Global Phenomenon

Bad customer service isn't just an American problem. It's a global export.

I've consulted for companies in 23 countries across 6 continents. The details vary, but the patterns are remarkably consistent:

Developed countries: Over-invested in technology that replaces humans, under-invested in humans who can actually solve problems

Developing countries: Used as offshore customer service centers for companies that don't want to pay developed-world wages for developed-world problems

Authoritarian countries: Customer service reflects the general relationship between institutions and individuals bureaucratic, opaque, and designed to discourage complaints

Democratic countries: Customer service has been captured by short-term financial incentives that override long-term relationship building

The specific technologies vary. The cultural expressions of frustration are different. But the underlying economics are the same everywhere: companies have learned they can take customers' money while systematically avoiding responsibility for customer satisfaction.

The Generational Divide That Isn't

There's a myth that younger generations prefer digital customer service while older generations want human interaction.

That's not what the data shows.

When the stakes are high, when money is involved, when something important is broken, when time is critical every generation prefers human customer service. Gen Z may be comfortable with chatbots for simple questions, but they want humans for complex problems just like everyone else.

The difference isn't generational preference. It's learned helplessness.

Younger customers have been trained from an early age that human customer service doesn't work, so they don't expect it. They've adapted to systems designed to avoid them by developing workarounds, gaming the algorithms, and accepting that most customer service interactions will be frustrating.

Older customers remember when customer service was personal and effective. They haven't yet accepted that the degradation is permanent.

But both generations are equally frustrated when the digital systems fail them. Both want human help when chatbots can't solve their problems. Both feel betrayed when companies promise support they don't deliver.

The Political Unifier

There are not many issues that unite this country across political lines, but frustration with customer service is certainly one of them.

Republicans and Democrats disagree about the role of government, but they both hate dealing with government customer service.

Progressives and conservatives have different views on corporate regulation, but they both get frustrated when corporations treat them with contempt.

Urban and rural Americans have different economic challenges, but they both struggle with the same cable companies and phone providers.

Customer service failure is the rare issue that creates genuine bipartisan fury. Everyone has been trapped in phone tree hell. Everyone has dealt with chatbots that can't understand simple requests. Everyone has been transferred between departments that can't see each other's information.

If politicians wanted to find an issue with universal appeal, customer service reform would be it. But most politicians never experience the customer service systems that torment their constituents.

They have staff who handle their personal customer service issues. They have corporate accounts with dedicated relationship managers. They get whisked past the normal customer experience straight to VIP treatment.

So they don't feel the pain personally, and it rarely becomes a political priority.

The Democracy of Misery

In most areas of life, money can buy you a better experience. First-class flights, private healthcare, concierge services wealth provides options.

But customer service is remarkably democratic in its awfulness. Even wealthy customers get trapped in the same phone trees, deal with the same chatbots, and navigate the same policies as everyone else.

Sure, some companies offer premium support tiers. But those are exceptions that prove the rule. For most interactions with most companies, everyone gets the same terrible experience regardless of how much money they spend.

A millionaire calling to dispute a credit card charge gets the same hold music as a minimum-wage worker. A Fortune 500 CEO trying to cancel a subscription faces the same retention specialist gauntlet as a college student.

The technology doesn't discriminate. The policies apply equally. The frustration is universal.

The Isolation Paradox

Modern customer service creates a strange paradox: we're all having the same terrible experiences, but we're having them alone.

In the old days, you dealt with customer service in person, often in front of other customers. When a merchant treated you badly, other people saw it. When you got great service, others witnessed that too.

There was a social element to customer service that created natural accountability and shared experience.

Now you deal with customer service in isolation. You're alone on hold, alone with the chatbot, alone with your frustration. When something goes wrong, it feels personal even when it's obviously systematic.

You don't see the hundreds of other customers having the exact same problem at the exact same time. You don't witness the service representative dealing with identical complaints all day long. You don't realize that your "unique" situation is actually a predictable result of broken systems.

This isolation makes customers feel powerless and companies feel unaccountable. Your individual complaint disappears into a database where it becomes a statistic rather than a story.

The Solution That Isn't

Companies have learned to respond to universal customer service complaints with universal customer service surveys.

Every interaction ends with: "Please take a moment to rate your experience."

But those surveys aren't designed to measure your actual experience. They're designed to generate favorable ratings that executives can point to when questioned about service quality.

The surveys arrive immediately after interactions, before you've had time to discover whether the "solution" actually worked. They use rating scales that overestimate "satisfied" customers.

The result: companies can report improving customer satisfaction scores while customer satisfaction actually plummets.

The surveys create the illusion that companies are listening while actually helping them avoid listening.

The Pain That Unites Us

What makes the universal pain of customer service so significant isn't just that everyone experiences it. It's that everyone knows it doesn't have to be this way.

We've all had good customer service experiences. Rare, memorable moments when someone actually helped us quickly and effectively. When a representative had authority to solve problems and seemed to care about solving them. When technology made things easier instead of harder.

Those experiences prove that good customer service is possible. They're not miracles or accidents, they're glimpses of what customer service could be if companies chose to prioritize it.

The universal pain exists because companies have universally chosen short-term cost optimization over long-term relationship building. They've all read the same consultant reports, implemented the same cost-cutting measures, and deployed the same deflection technologies.

The pain is universal because the solutions are universal. And those solutions are failing universally.

But here's the thing about universal problems: they create opportunities for universal solutions.

If everyone is frustrated with customer service, then everyone is ready for something better. If every company is using the same broken playbook, then any company that breaks from that playbook has a massive competitive advantage.

The universal pain of customer service isn't just a problem to be solved. It's a market opportunity waiting to be seized by companies brave enough to honor the promises they make.

The question is: who will be first to break ranks with the industry consensus that customers should be avoided rather than served?

And what will it take for customers to demand and reward that change?

PART II

HOW WE GOT HERE

"From Personal to Systematic" *How customer service evolved from human accountability to corporate avoidance*

CHAPTER 2

HOW WE GOT HERE

Era 1: Personal Commerce (Ancient - 1850)

The social contract I described in Chapter 1 wasn't always broken. For most of human history, customer service worked because the incentives were aligned. Merchants who treated customers badly went out of business. Customers who cheated merchants got blacklisted from the marketplace.

It was simple, direct, and effective.

Let me show you how we got from there to here.

Hammurabi's Precedent

The story of customer service begins around 1750 BC with the Code of Hammurabi, the first time anyone bothered to write down rules about how merchants should treat customers.

To be clear, Hammurabi's Code was brutal. It mentions the death penalty 30 times. It was paternalistic and doesn't hold up well to modern standards, think the Old Testament without the promise of salvation. But it did three critical things that still influence customer service today.

First, it established that there would be accountability any time there was a perceived wrong done to a customer. This was revolutionary. For the first time in human history, we had clear consequences for merchants who didn't deliver on their promises of quality and service. If a merchant sold bad grain, cheated on weights, or failed to deliver what was promised, there were specific punishments.

Second, it created tiers of customers. There was a three-tier system: upper class, middle class, and lower class. Different punishments for harming different types of customers. Sound familiar? All customers are equal, but some are more equal than others, a principle that still governs customer service today.

Third, it published these rules on a stone tablet for all to see. This level of transparency was a game changer. We take for granted that policies are displayed prominently for all to see, but this was the first time anyone had done it. No more secret rules or arbitrary merchant decisions.

But here's what's most important about Hammurabi's Code: it worked because everyone involved had skin in the game. Merchants lived in the same communities as their customers. They shopped in each other's stores. Their children played together. Their reputations were everything.

A merchant couldn't screw over a customer and disappear into anonymity. Everyone knew who the merchant was and how they did business.

Medieval Quality Focus

Fast forward to the Middle Ages, and trade had become more sophisticated but the fundamental dynamics remained the same. Medieval commerce was built around a simple principle: if merchants made quality goods and treated customers fairly, most complaints could be avoided entirely.

This was the prevailing theory of customer service: prevent problems rather than solve them.

When problems did arise, they were handled in person through direct interactions between merchants and customers. There were no corporate policies, no phone trees, no customer service departments. Just two people working out a problem face to face.

The very wealthy might use letters for communication, but they were the exception. Most commerce happened in person, in the moment, with immediate resolution.

This personal approach had built-in accountability. The merchant had to look the customer in the eye when explaining why something went wrong. The customer had to face the merchant when making a complaint. Both parties were motivated to find reasonable solutions because they'd likely see each other again.

Over time, we used our ears a lot less and our eyes a lot more to understand the world. The printing press in the late Middle Ages began this shift. We started seeing the world in more binary terms than our ancestors wrote rules instead of spoken agreements, documented policies instead of personal relationships.

This would have big implications for customer service in the centuries to come.

The Merchant's Dilemma

For thousands of years, merchants faced what I call the merchant's dilemma: they HAD to provide good service because they had no other choice.

In a world before mass marketing, before advertising, before brand awareness campaigns, there was only one way to grow a business: word of mouth. And word of mouth was entirely dependent on how merchants treated customers.

Think about it: if you were a blacksmith in a village of 500 people, your reputation was literally everything. Shoe a horse poorly, and everyone would know about it by sunset. Overcharge for your work, and your customers would tell their neighbors. Refuse to fix a mistake, and you'd be out of business within a month.

There was no corporate headquarters to hide behind. No customer service department to deflect complaints to. No legal team to write policies that protected you from accountability.

Just the merchant, their customers, and their reputation.

This created powerful incentives for good service:

Immediate consequences: Bad service meant immediate loss of business. There was no quarterly grace period, no time to "turn things around." Merchants fixed problems immediately or lost customers immediately.

Community accountability: Everyone knew everyone else's business. Merchants couldn't afford to have even a few unhappy customers because they'd poison the well for everyone else.

Limited customer base: Merchants couldn't afford to lose customers because there weren't unlimited replacement customers. In a village of 500 people, maybe 50 needed their services. Lose 10 customers to bad service, and they'd lost 20% of their market.

Personal relationships: Merchants weren't just serving customers they were serving neighbors, friends, community members. It's hard to treat someone badly when you see them at church every Sunday.

This wasn't altruism. This was survival.

The merchant's dilemma created what we'd now call perfect market conditions for customer service. The incentives were completely aligned: good service meant business success, bad service meant business failure.

The Dutch East India Company: Distance Changes Everything

Even as commerce became more sophisticated and global, the fundamental principles of personal accountability persisted well into the 1600s.

Take the Dutch East India Company, the most powerful company on Earth in its time. It launched fleets, negotiated with kings, and charted new trade routes in a world still being mapped. It was big, bold, and deeply serious about business.

And yet, for all its power, the most critical part of that business communicating with customers moved at the speed of wind and weather.

If you had a complaint, a suggestion, or even just a question, you wrote it down, sealed it with wax, and handed it to a captain. The reply might arrive in four months if the sea behaved, the ship didn't sink, and someone on the other end read your letter. More likely, it was a year. Sometimes, never.

There was no call center. No chatbot. No hold music. Just ink, salt air, and a long wait.

But here's what's remarkable: they cared about the work. They tracked cargo meticulously. Kept records by hand in vast ledgers. Filed every letter.

They built systems to manage vast operations that stretched from Amsterdam to Ceylon.

When Hendrik van Loon, a merchant stationed in Batavia, received dried cod instead of the saffron he'd ordered, he sat down and wrote a detailed letter explaining the issue. He sealed it with wax and sent it on the next ship bound for Amsterdam.

Four months later, his letter reached a clerk. It was logged, reviewed, and a response was drafted with care: an apology, an explanation, and instructions for a corrected shipment. It was sent back the way it came another four months by boat.

By the time it arrived, Hendrik had already adjusted. Found a local buyer. Swapped the cod. Moved on. He had no choice.

But here's the strange paradox: in that world, the biggest challenge was speed, not intent. Information traveled slowly. Mistakes took months to fix. But everyone from the captain to the clerk was doing their best within a system that had hard limits.

The VOC had slow service, but meaningful intent. Time was the enemy, not the company.

Today, speed is solved. We can communicate instantly. File a complaint in seconds. Get a refund before breakfast. But in fixing speed, we've broken something else: the deliberation, the care, the feeling that someone is actually reading the message instead of just acknowledging it with an automated "We're on it."

The End of an Era

For most of human history, customer service worked because it had to work. Merchants and customers were connected by geography, community, and mutual dependence. The incentives were perfectly aligned: treat customers well and prosper, treat them badly and fail.

But this system had built-in limitations. It couldn't scale beyond personal relationships. It couldn't handle mass production. It couldn't support global commerce.

Personal commerce worked beautifully for small communities with limited product choices and direct relationships between buyers and sellers. But it was about to run headlong into the Industrial Revolution.

Mass production was going to break the personal connection between merchants and customers forever. The question was: would we find a way to maintain accountability and incentive alignment at scale?

Spoiler alert: we would try. For a while, we'd even succeed. But the seeds of our current customer service crisis were about to be planted in the factories and assembly lines of the Industrial Age.

Personal commerce worked because everyone was accountable to everyone else. The Industrial Revolution was about to change that forever.

Next: Era 2 - Industrial Separation (1850-1920): How mass production broke the personal link, but incentives stayed aligned.

Era 2: Industrial Separation (1850-1920)

The Industrial Revolution didn't just change how things were made, it changed who was responsible when those things didn't work.

For the first time in human history, the person who made your product had never met you. The person who sold it to you might not know how it was made. And the person who handled your complaint definitely wasn't the person who could fix the underlying problem.

Personal accountability was about to become corporate responsibility. And corporate responsibility, as we'd learn, is no one's responsibility.

Mass Production Changes Everything

The 19th century brought specialization and mass production on a scale the world had never seen. As goods were mass-produced and sold at scale, the personalization of making goods with a specific customer in mind began to disappear.

Products were no longer made for John the baker or Mary the seamstress. They were produced for a TBD customer to be determined later, at the point of sale, by someone who had nothing to do with manufacturing.

This broke the direct link between maker and user that had governed commerce for millennia.

Under the old system, if a craftsman made a bad shoe, the customer brought it back to them. The craftsman had to look the customer in the eye and explain what went wrong. They had to make it right because their reputation and their livelihood depended on it.

Under the new system, if a factory made a bad shoe, the customer brought it back to a retailer who brought it back to a distributor who might eventually mention it to the manufacturer. By the time the feedback reached the person who could actually fix the problem, it had been filtered through multiple layers of bureaucracy and stripped of all human context.

The industrial age created the first customer service departments not because companies suddenly cared more about service, but because they needed someone to handle the complaints that could no longer be resolved by the person who made the product.

Customer service became mass-produced for a TBD customer, just like everything else.

But here's what's crucial to understand: the incentive for companies to provide great customer service was still very strong. Customer service was still their marketing and sales. Companies failed at customer service, and word of mouth would still kill their business.

The Industrial Revolution broke the personal link between maker and customer, but it didn't break the business imperative to keep customers happy.

Marketing Becomes Its Own Beast

The separation of production from customer relationships created space for something new: marketing as a distinct business function.

In 1879, James Norris Gamble, chemist and son of Procter & Gamble, created a soap and mass-marketed it as Ivory Soap famously "99.44% pure it floats." The campaign combined scientific-sounding language with biblical branding.

For the first time, we see mass marketing detached from the utility of the product and detached from service but focused on managing perception.

This was revolutionary. For thousands of years, the only way to build demand for products was to make good products and treat customers well. Word of mouth was the marketing department.

But Ivory Soap proved companies could create demand through messaging, imagery, and emotional manipulation independent of product quality or service experience.

The most dramatic example came in the 1920s. Lambert Pharmaceuticals was an unknown company until Gerald Lambert, son of the owner, had an idea. He wanted to improve sales of Listerine, and instead of relying on word of mouth, he did something groundbreaking.

He framed bad breath not as an inconvenience but as a "medical condition" "halitosis." Then he ran ads depicting a woman who could never find a husband due to her "halitosis."

Just like that, a faster, more effective form of revenue generation was born. Instead of waiting for the slow wheels of word of mouth, companies could use mass media to manufacture demand by manipulating customer emotions.

Marketing created urgency around a problem the company invented.

It worked. In 6 years, Lambert had gone from $100,000 in Listerine sales to $4,000,000. Lambert would later lament in his memoirs that he wanted his epitaph to read: "Here lies the body of the Father of Halitosis."

Marketing didn't just sell products; it started manufacturing problems. With mass media at its fingertips, it could create urgency out of thin air.

In 1930, Procter & Gamble started sponsoring radio dramas aimed at housewives. Each episode overtly promoted their soap products like Oxydol and Duz. The term "soap opera" literally came from this tactic.

Marketing was not only being industrialized it was making customer service less relevant. Companies could build emotional ties to customers at scale without ever having to deliver on those emotional promises through actual service experiences.

Marketing had learned to work independently of service.

The Last Aligned Era

But here's what's important: even though marketing could now work independently of service, service was still the most reliable way to grow a business.

In 1868, Watkins Liniment gave us the first customer satisfaction guarantee: "If you're not satisfied, your money back." This wasn't marketing fluff, it was business strategy.

Companies discovered that standing behind their products with guarantees actually increased sales. Customers were more willing to try new products if they knew they could get their money back if things went wrong.

The guarantee wasn't just about handling complaints it was about preventing them. Companies knew that if they had to refund money to too many customers, they'd go out of business. So, they worked harder to make products that wouldn't need returning.

This created a virtuous cycle: better products led to fewer complaints, which led to lower refund costs, which led to higher profits, which could be invested in even better products.

Even with mass production and mass marketing, the fundamental equation still held good service and good products were the most reliable path to business success.

Word of mouth was still the most powerful marketing force. A satisfied customer might tell three friends. A dissatisfied customer would tell ten. Companies couldn't afford to have too many people in the "tell ten friends" category.

The incentives were still aligned. Investing in customer service was investing in business growth.

But this alignment was fragile. It depended on word of mouth remaining the primary driver of customer acquisition. And that was about to change.

The Technology Revolution Begins

In 1876, Alexander Graham Bell invented the telephone, but it didn't immediately catch on. The real game-changer would come later.

The telephone promised to solve the biggest problem with industrial-scale customer service: distance. For the first time, customers and companies could have real-time conversations without being in the same place.

Early telephone systems required human operators, usually women to manually connect calls by plugging cables into the right sockets. It was personal service delivered through technology.

But even in these early days, there were two competing visions for how telephone technology should serve customers:

The Bell Vision: Human-centered service where operators provided personalized assistance. Bell wanted to make using the phone as easy as possible for customers. You picked up the phone, told the operator what you wanted, and she made it happen.

The Independent Vision: Automated systems that reduced costs and eliminated human error. Customers would do more of the work themselves, but the service would be faster and cheaper.

This tension between human service versus automated efficiency would define customer service for the next century and a half.

For now, Bell's vision won. Human operators remained the standard for decades because early customers valued personal assistance over automation. Companies competed on the quality of their operators, not the sophistication of their technology.

The telephone was seen as a tool to provide better customer service at scale, not to avoid providing customer service altogether.

The Foundation for Everything

By 1920, all the pieces were in place for modern customer service:

Industrial production had broken the direct link between makers and customers, creating the need for specialized customer service functions.

Mass marketing had proven that companies could build demand independent of service quality, reducing the immediate business pressure to provide great service.

Telephone technology had created the possibility of serving customers at scale without face-to-face interaction.

Corporate structure had separated ownership from management, allowing decisions to be made by people who would never meet the customers affected by those decisions.

But the fundamental incentives were still aligned. Companies that provided good service still grew faster than companies that didn't. Word of mouth was still the most powerful marketing force. Customer satisfaction was still the most reliable predictor of business success.

The tools existed to scale customer service in ways that would either preserve the personal accountability of the merchant era or destroy it entirely.

For the next 70 years, we'd try to preserve it. Companies would use technology to provide better human service at scale. They'd invest in customer service as a competitive advantage. They'd treat customer satisfaction as a leading indicator of business health.

It would be the golden age of customer service, an era when "the customer is always right" wasn't just a slogan but a business strategy that actually made sense.

But even during this golden age, the seeds of our current crisis were being planted. The same forces that made better service possible technology, scale, corporate structure would eventually make worse service more profitable.

Mass production broke the personal connection, but good service was still the best way to grow a business. Technology was about to change that calculation forever.

Next: Era 3 - The Telephone Revolution (1880-1970): How technology was used to enhance human service at scale

Era 3: The Telephone Revolution (1880s-1970s)

I n 1876, Alexander Graham Bell spoke the first words ever transmitted by telephone: "Mr. Watson, come here, I want to see you."

He had no idea he was launching the industrialization of customer service.

For 4,000 years, customer service had been fundamentally local and personal. When Nanni had a problem with Ea-nasir's copper, he carved his complaint into clay and hand-delivered it. The merchant and customer lived in the same city, shopped in the same marketplace, and faced each other as human beings.

The telephone changed everything. For the first time in human history, companies could serve customers they would never meet, in places they would never visit, through conversations that left no permanent record.

Distance, which had always been customer service's greatest limitation, suddenly became its greatest asset.

The Operator's Promise

In the early days of telephony, customer service actually improved. When you wanted to make a call, you picked up the receiver and spoke to a human operator—usually a woman—who would personally connect your call.

These operators became the first industrialized customer service representatives. They were trained to be polite, efficient, and helpful. They knew their customers by voice. They remembered who called whom regularly. They provided information about numbers, directions, even time and weather.

The Bell System built its reputation on the quality of these human interactions. "Number, please?" became the friendliest phrase in American commerce.

This was customer service at scale that still felt personal. Technology was used to connect customers to humans, not to avoid them.

The Strowger Revolution

The system worked beautifully until Almon Brown Strowger, an undertaker in Kansas City, discovered that his business was suffering because a telephone operator was married to his competitor and was routing his calls to her husband's funeral home.

Strowger's response was swift and revolutionary: he invented the automatic switchboard.

No more operators. No more human intermediaries who could play favorites or make "mistakes." Just dial the number and get connected directly.

When Strowger tried to sell his automatic telephone switch to Bell, they didn't even reply. Bell executives believed that human-centered service with women operators was superior to any machine.

They were right, but they were also naive about what the future would choose.

The Two Philosophies

From 1890 to 1930, two competing visions of customer service battled for supremacy:

Bell's Vision: Human-centered service where customers received personal attention from trained operators who made the technology invisible and the experience effortless.

Strowger's Vision: Automated efficiency where customers did more work themselves but got faster, cheaper, more reliable service.

Bell argued that automatic systems put more work onto customers, who had to dial numbers themselves instead of simply telling an operator what they wanted. Bell wanted to make using the phone as easy as possible for customers.

Independent phone companies promoted automation's benefits: confidentiality, reduced costs, and avoidance of operators' mistakes. Customers sometimes blamed operators for missed calls and wrong numbers.

The debate wasn't really about technology. It was about philosophy: Should customer service prioritize human connection or operational efficiency?

The Resistance

Even as automation advanced, there was significant pushback. In 1930, Senator Carter Glass of Virginia introduced a resolution banning dial phones, arguing that he objected to being "transformed into one of the employees of the telephone company without compensation."

President Hoover banned automatic phones from the White House in 1929, preferring human-based telephone service.

These weren't Luddites afraid of technology. They were people who understood that automation shifted work from companies to customers while eliminating the human relationships that made business personal.

But the economic advantages of automation were too compelling to resist.

The Automatic Call Distributor

The match toward automation accelerated with the invention of the Automatic Call Distributor (ACD) in the 1950s. For the first time in history, anyone could call any company and be automatically routed to someone who could help them.

Rockwell built the first commercial ACD for Continental Airlines to take more reservations without hiring hundreds of operators to route calls. The technology was about getting customers to human-based customer service more efficiently.

This was the sweet spot: automation behind the scenes, humans on the front lines.

The incentive alignment between customers and companies was still intact. Providing great human-based service was good for customers and good for companies. The technology made human service more accessible, not less human.

The Call Center Is Born

By the 1960s, companies like Birmingham Press and Mail in Britain set up teams to take catalog orders by phone—some of the first real call centers. These were rooms full of people taking down what customers wanted so someone could send it to them.

American corporations realized phones meant they didn't need physical stores everywhere. They could centralize service, cut costs, control the narrative, and maybe hide from angry customers in distant cities.

Then in 1967, AT&T gave us the 1-800 number, allowing customers to dial companies directly for free. Catalog sales boomed. Customer service departments followed.

Suddenly, you could call any company for free. It felt revolutionary.

The Economics of Scale

The telephone era brought customer service its first taste of genuine economies of scale. Instead of training one clerk in each store, companies could train specialists in centralized call centers. Instead of maintaining local expertise everywhere, they could concentrate knowledge in a few locations.

For customers, this often meant better service. The person answering your call about a technical problem might actually understand the product, unlike the local store clerk who sold everything from shoes to soup.

Companies could offer 24-hour service without keeping stores open all night. They could provide consistent service regardless of which location you called. They could track customer interactions and build relationships across multiple touchpoints.

This was industrialization in service of better customer experience.

The Warning Signs

But even in this golden age, the seeds of future problems were visible to those who looked carefully.

The operator replacement pattern: As automatic switching eliminated telephone operators—from 324,000 in the 1920s to 40,000 in the 1980s—companies learned that customers would accept doing more work themselves if the trade-off was faster, cheaper service.

The centralization trade-off: Moving customer service to call centers meant representatives had less local knowledge and personal connection to customers. They could solve more types of problems but knew less about individual customers' specific situations.

The metrics mindset: Call centers introduced the first systematic measurement of customer service: calls per hour, average handle time, resolution rates. What got measured got managed, and what got managed got optimized.

The cost center mentality: As customer service moved from local profit centers (stores that sold products and provided service) to centralized cost centers (departments that only provided service), the economic incentives began to shift.

The Technology Trap

The telephone era proved that technology could enhance customer service, but it also established a dangerous precedent: customers would accept increased complexity and self-service in exchange for increased access and reduced cost.

Every time customers accepted dialing their own numbers instead of asking operators, they were training companies that automation was acceptable. Every time they navigated phone trees instead of speaking directly to humans, they were teaching businesses that efficiency could trump relationship.

The technology wasn't the problem. The technology was remarkable. The problem was that it created possibilities for both better service and cheaper service, and companies were starting to learn they didn't have to choose better.

The End of an Era

The telephone era lasted roughly 80 years, from 1880 to 1960. For most of that time, it represented customer service's finest hour: human connection enhanced by technology, personal relationships maintained at industrial scale, customer needs balanced with operational efficiency.

But by the 1960s, new technologies and new economic pressures were emerging. Computer systems promised even greater automation. Global markets created new competitive pressures. Financial markets began demanding quarterly growth that prioritized short-term profits over long-term relationships.

The stage was set for the next revolution in customer service—one that would prioritize efficiency over emotion, cost-cutting over relationship-building, and shareholder value over customer satisfaction.

The telephone had taught companies they could serve customers at a distance. The next era would teach them they could avoid customers at a distance too.

The Lessons We Forgot

The telephone era offers crucial lessons for modern customer service:

Technology should enhance human connection, not replace it. The most successful telephone-era companies used automation to connect customers to humans more efficiently, not to avoid human contact entirely.

Customers will accept complexity in exchange for value. People learned to dial their own numbers because it gave them faster, more reliable connections. But the complexity must deliver genuine customer benefit, not just company cost savings.

Centralization can improve service quality while reducing costs. Call centers allowed companies to provide specialized expertise and extended hours without the overhead of local offices. But centralization only works when it maintains the quality of individual customer relationships.

Measurement drives behavior. The metrics that began in the telephone era—calls per hour, handle time, resolution rates—shaped how customer service evolved. Companies that measured customer satisfaction alongside operational efficiency created better systems than those that focused only on internal metrics.

Scale requires systematic training and quality control. The telephone era companies that succeeded invested heavily in training their representatives and maintaining consistent service standards. Those that treated call center jobs as unskilled labor created the template for modern customer service failures.

The Bridge to Modernity

The telephone era was the bridge between personal, local customer service and the industrial, global systems we have today. It proved that customer service could be scaled without losing its humanity.

But it also created the tools and techniques that would later be used to industrialize customer avoidance rather than customer service.

The next era would take the telephone era's innovations—centralization, automation, systematic measurement, and cost optimization—and use them to serve companies rather than customers.

The transition didn't happen overnight. It happened gradually, one optimization at a time, one cost-cutting measure at a time, one technological "improvement" at a time.

By the time customers realized what had been lost, the companies had already moved on to the next cost-saving innovation.

The telephone era ended not with a bang but with a busy signal. And when customers finally got through, they found themselves talking to machines designed to sound human while serving entirely inhuman purposes.

The golden age of customer service was over. The age of customer avoidance was about to begin.

Era 4: Digital Transformation (1990-Present)

For seven decades, technology had made human service better. The internet promised to continue that trend. Instead, it marked the beginning of the end.

The same tools that could have created the most responsive, personalized, efficient customer service in human history became weapons of mass deflection. Not because the technology was bad, but because the economic incentives had finally shifted decisively against customer service.

This is the era when helping customers became the enemy of helping shareholders.

The Internet's False Promise

I remember my first tech support email. I was a college student, my dial-up modem sounded like a dying robot, and my AOL connection kept dropping. I emailed the ISP support desk with what I thought was a brilliant, well-reasoned technical plea.

Four days later, I got back what can only be described as a digital shrug: "Try rebooting your modem."

That was the customer service revolution of the 1990s.

The internet ushered in email, FAQs, web forms, and the earliest live chats. Each promised faster, more convenient ways for customers to get help. Each also spectacularly underdelivered at first.

Email was supposed to be the great equalizer. By the late '90s, any company with a website slapped a support email address on it. Customers thought, "Finally, no more waiting on hold!"

The reality? Companies treated email like snail mail with an @ symbol. Replies took days. Responses were copy-paste masterpieces of vagueness. Still, for people like me who despised call center hold music, email felt miraculous.

But the adoption of email wasn't driven by customer preference, it was driven by cost. Email was cheaper than phone support and faster than mailing letters back and forth. Companies didn't need call centers full of reps; they just needed a few people with keyboards and decent grammar.

The scale that email offered big and small companies to deliver customer service without exploding costs made this a fast-growing channel. At first, customers liked it. But as it became more popular, email became just another channel with long waits and increasingly impersonal responses.

For one thing, customers would send the same email about the same issue multiple times sometimes due to impatience, sometimes because it was unclear if anyone had received their message. Consultants came up with autoresponders that gave customers confidence their inquiry was being reviewed.

These autoresponders just created even more emails. Eventually, email became a channel universally hated by all. Companies hated it because it was inefficient. Customers hated it because it was ineffective.

Email was on its deathbed; it just proved difficult to kill.

The Self-Service Trap

The next logical step was an even cheaper option: self-service.

FAQs became the next adventure. In theory, they empowered customers to solve their own problems at 2 AM. In practice, they became digital graveyards where answers went to die.

The good news: when self-service worked, it really worked. Maggie's Muffins, a local bakery, was drowning in calls. "Are you open on Sundays?" "Do you have gluten-free options?" "Do your muffins have real blueberries?" Maggie put those answers online and suddenly calls dropped 60%. Her staff went back to baking instead of fielding existential muffin questions.

The bad news: most FAQ sections were written by people who had never answered a customer question and designed by people who had never had a customer problem.

Search for "how to cancel my subscription" and you'd find articles about "managing your account preferences" and "updating billing information" and "temporarily pausing service" everything except actually canceling.

These help centers weren't designed to help. They were designed to exhaust you. The theory was that if you spent 20 minutes reading unhelpful articles, you might solve your problem yourself, give up entirely, or at least be too tired to complain when you finally reached a human.

Web forms followed the online suggestion boxes of the '90s. You'd fill out a clunky form, hit submit, and pray someone read it. No confirmation. No tracking number. No follow-up.

Digital self-service was going so badly that companies decided to reintroduce human support, but instead of using the telephone, they wanted something cheaper I mean, more efficient. Enter live chat.

Live chat arrived at the end of the '90s and felt like magic when it worked. A human (or what you hoped was a human) typed back answers in real time. It was glorious.

The problem? Most companies never had agents online when you needed them. You'd click "Chat Now" only to see "No agents available" every time you actually needed help.

The Phone Tree Forest

While the internet was busy disappointing everyone, the telephone system was evolving too in the wrong direction.

I don't call 1-800 numbers in front of children anymore. I don't recommend you do either. I end up yelling "customer service" at a machine that's programmed to ignore me.

The phone tree started simple in the 1970s: "Press 1 for billing, 2 for technical support." Then it grew. And grew. And grew.

By the 2000s, it had become a labyrinth with no exit. A phone maze that yells "Sorry, I didn't get that" every time you try to escape using human language.

The IVR (Interactive Voice Response) system was supposed to help you. Instead, it locked you in. Your call was deemed "low value" translation: not worth a person's time.

I once audited an IVR system that handled 24 million calls a year. It was awful. Truly, catastrophically awful. The executive who ran it bragged about saving $50 million annually.

"Do you want to make it better?" I asked.

He looked confused. "Why? The system works."

And there it was. The perfect summary of digital-era customer service technology: it works perfectly for the company. The fact that it tortures customers is not a bug, it's a feature.

The goal wasn't better service. It was cheaper service, and better service would just be incidental.

The goal of phone automation was something called "deflection" and "containment". I call it what it is: digital dodgeball. The former is to avoid talking to you altogether; the latter is about keeping you trapped in automation for as long as you can bear it.

The Outsourcing Acceleration

Just when you thought domestic customer service couldn't get worse, companies discovered they could export the problem to other countries.

My first time in Bogotá, I got picked up by a guy holding a sign with my name. Felt like a VIP until we climbed into a black SUV flanked by men with AK-47s. The driver told me to roll up my window. He said guys on motorbikes were known to slice off wrists for a nice watch.

Why was I there? Not to cure cancer. I was there to find cheaper labor. To save a few bucks on customer service.

Companies don't want to talk to you. If they have to, they want to do it as cheaply as possible. U.S. wages were too high. So, they sent the jobs overseas.

It started in the '90s with India. Good English, but the accents made customers rage. That didn't matter. Companies didn't care about how it felt, only what it cost.

Then the Philippines and Eastern Europe became customer service hubs. On paper, it was smart: lower wages, 24/7 coverage, scalable talent pools.

But something got lost in translation literally and metaphorically. Cultural nuances, accents, and a lack of true authority turned most reps into polite gatekeepers with no keys.

Picture this: a telecom customer in Texas calls about a billing issue. The rep in Manila says she can't help. The customer yells. The call escalates to a supervisor... in Kansas, 2 hours later. The supervisor issues a $10 credit after 2.5 hours of customer torture.

I even built software to help call center reps "neutralize" their accents. I thought it would be a hit. And in some ways, it was. But the real success wasn't fixing the problem, it was ignoring it while saving money.

Outsourcing is everywhere now. I've flown to Africa, Southeast Asia, and South America, all in search of cheaper labor. I've been to beautiful places that only made sense to the CFO. "Paradise but make it cheap."

Nobody loves it, not customers, not workers. But it continues because cost is king. Even when it hurts the experience. Even when customers complain. Companies keep outsourcing because it's cheaper.

They treat customer service like a chore. Like cleaning your room. Do just enough to say you did it.

Social Media's Brief, Shining Moment

There was a moment, brief, beautiful when customer service on social media felt like magic.

You tweeted about your broken blender or your canceled flight, and poof: someone from the company responded. Quickly. Publicly. Maybe even helpfully.

It felt like we, the people, had finally found the back door into the customer service department.

And for a while, we did.

Back in the 2010s, companies fell in love with social media as a way to talk to customers. Why? Because it was fast, cheap, and very, very public.

If you complained loud enough, someone would usually show up and try to make it right if only to avoid being roasted by the internet.

Picture this: You're at the airport. Flight canceled. Nobody at the counter knows anything. So, you tweet: "Hey @FlyRightAir, what's the deal?!" Three minutes later: "We're on it! Rebooked you, drink vouchers at Gate 9."

You felt powerful. The system worked. And you didn't even have to talk to anyone.

Behind the scenes, companies loved this setup too. Talking to you on Twitter cost them about a dollar. Phone calls? Six times that.

And let's be honest, if you're a big brand and can replace a call center with one guy in a hoodie and a browser tab, you're going to try.

It wasn't just cheap; it made them look good. Every helpful response was public. Every fix was a tiny PR win.

But the party couldn't last. When more customers started using social media for support, the economics changed. The algorithms were no longer boosting routine customer service responses for the world to see. Instead, they seemed to only amplify the negative complaints.

Many company policies and practices aren't exactly popular, so using social media for customer service now had limited upside and unlimited downside. The channel got defunded and de-emphasized, reverting to being mainly a marketing channel.

The Omnichannel Shell Game

All of these new ways of contacting customer service created a new problem: if you've ever repeated your issue three times to three different people on three different platforms, you understand this well.

The consultants came up with something called "omnichannel."

It was supposed to be a revolution in customer service. One smooth experience, no matter how you reached out. Call, email, live chat, tweet the same story, same support, no bouncing around.

In reality? It's been like trying to get a refund from a haunted vending machine.

You email about a broken product. Nothing. You call. "Can you explain the issue?" You scream. Again. The agent has zero context. You start from scratch.

You ask about returns on Instagram. They send you to email. Email sends you to a phone line. The phone sends you to therapy.

What happened? Each team uses a different system. They can't see what the others are doing. You're not being helped, you're being passed around like a hot potato with Wi-Fi.

Omnichannel was supposed to be the fix. It was sold as "One support experience, no matter how you contact us!" Instead, we got "One issue, five channels, seven explanations, and zero resolution."

It cost companies millions. It gave customers more ways to get frustrated.

You didn't ask for omnichannel. You just wanted help. A person. Who knows your issue. And could fix it.

Instead, we got customer service Whac-A-Mole.

The COVID Acceleration

The pandemic accelerated every bad trend in customer service technology. Companies had legitimate reasons to reduce human contact, but they used the crisis as cover for changes they wanted to make anyway.

"Due to COVID-19, we're experiencing higher than normal call volumes. Please visit our website for faster service."

That message is still playing in 2025, five years after the pandemic ended.

COVID became the excuse for permanent degradation of human service, wrapped in public health language but motivated by cost reduction.

The Breaking Point

By 2025, we had the most sophisticated customer service technology in history and the worst customer service experience.

We could track packages in real-time but couldn't reach a human who cared about our problem. We could video chat with people on the other side of the world but couldn't get our internet provider to answer the phone. We had AI that could write poetry but chatbots that couldn't understand "I want to cancel my subscription."

The technology worked perfectly. The incentives were completely broken.

Every innovation that should have made customer service better was used to make it cheaper instead. Every tool that could have enhanced human connection was deployed to avoid human contact.

For seven decades, technology had been the friend of customer service. Now it was the enemy.

Not because the technology was bad, but because the economic pressures finally overwhelmed the customer service imperative. Quarterly earnings became more important than customer relationships. Stock prices became more important than satisfaction scores. Deflection rates became more important than resolution rates.

The same technology that once connected customers and companies now keeps them apart. The tools haven't changed, but the goals have.

We didn't arrive at terrible customer service by accident. We engineered it, decision by decision, quarter by quarter, innovation by innovation.

The question is: how did the economics get so broken that every technological advance made the human experience worse?

To understand that we need to examine the brutal mathematics that drive every customer service decision in the modern economy.

Next: Chapter 3 - The Economics of Bad Service: Why the math behind customer service is designed to make you suffer

PART III

THE SYSTEM IN ACTION

Inside the economics, psychology, and technology of customer service failure

CHAPTER 3

THE ECONOMICS OF BAD SERVICE

Section 1: The Profit Motive

At a round table dinner in San Francisco a few years ago, I asked a room full of customer service executives what their vision of great customer service would look like.

The head of service for a large telco waxed poetic about "effortless service." Another executive talked about white glove treatment. A third said "delight." I let it go on for a minute as they all added specificity to their vision: seamless experiences, proactive outreach, customers hanging up satisfied instead of frustrated.

Beautiful stuff. Then I asked the follow-up question: "Are any of you close to that vision at your respective companies?"

Silence.

Every single one said no.

One executive let's call her Sarah said she had tried to make that vision a reality multiple times but couldn't. As she put it, "service transformation takes a lot of investment." Another CEO was more blunt: the business case didn't make sense. Good customer service, he said, didn't have the return on investment.

And there it was. The quiet part, said out loud.

These are some of the most powerful humans in customer service. They control budgets in the hundreds of millions. They have direct lines to CEOs. They understand what good service looks like, they want to deliver it, and they have the expertise to build it.

But the math says no.

The Customer Service Return on Investment Problem

Here's what that CEO meant when he said the business case didn't make sense:

Companies spend money on better service today. They might see results in 12-18 months. Maybe. If they can measure them. If other factors don't interfere. If the customers, they retain actually spend more money. If they refer new customers. If, if, if.

Meanwhile, companies spend money on marketing today, and they can track new customer acquisition by next week. Clean numbers. Clear attribution. Immediate revenue impact.

Guess which investment gets approved?

The problem isn't that executives don't care about customers. The problem is that caring about customers costs money this quarter, while the benefits show up in future quarters maybe. And most executives are measured on this quarter's performance.

The Math Is Brutal

Let me take you to Phoenix. It's 111 degrees and feels like someone parked a blow dryer outside the office. I'm in a stuffy glass cube with Carl, the VP of Customer Ops for a national appliance retailer. He's sweating not from the heat but from the realization that customers are abandoning his company like a sinking ship.

Carl's leaning over the table, red-faced, flipping through my report like it personally insulted him.

"These wait times," he mutters. "Eight minutes on average?"

"Actually, that's the good news," I say. "If you're over 50, it's twelve. Your IVR doesn't like old people."

Carl's chewing on the cap of a dry-erase marker. "So, what's the fix?"

I show him three options:

1. Hire more humans.

2. Invest in smarter automation.

3. Do a mix of both.

He barely glances at Option 1. "Nope. Too expensive."

Option 2, though? His eyes light up like it's Christmas. "Can we just route low-value stuff to bots?"

"Sure," I say. "If you're okay with a few more one-star Yelp reviews and some choice words on Reddit."

Carl doesn't laugh. I don't blame him.

Here's the truth: giving customers what they want, like not waiting forever costs real money. In Carl's case, fixing the issue with humans would cost an extra $12.4 million annually. That's 47 full-time customer service reps at $45K each, plus benefits, plus management overhead, plus training, plus the technology to support them.

$12.4 million to make customers happier.

But here's what Carl's CFO sees: $12.4 million that doesn't drive revenue growth. It doesn't increase market share. It doesn't create new product lines. It just... makes existing customers less angry.

And less angry doesn't show up on a quarterly earnings call.

Service as Insurance Claim

Here's the fundamental misunderstanding: most people think customer service is a product. Something you get when you buy something else.

It's not.

Customer service is a claim on a policy you didn't know you bought.

When you purchase a product or service, you're not just buying that product or service. You're also quietly buying an insurance policy with a promise that if something goes wrong, a human being somewhere will pick up the phone, solve your problem, and maybe even sound like they give a damn.

That's the unspoken agreement of commerce. Customer service is the claims department.

Let that sink in.

Most people still think of customer service as a "nice to have" bonus feature. But it's not. It's the payout mechanism. It's how companies deliver on the rest of the value proposition they dangled in front of you. When something breaks, ships late, misfires, or just doesn't work like it should, you're filing a claim on the policy you prepaid with your purchase.

And just like insurance companies, most businesses want to make damn sure they don't pay that claim if they can help it.

The Moment Money Changes Everything

Here's the math running in their heads:

They already have your money. From that moment on, every interaction with you is a cost. Not an opportunity. A cost.

And when you reach out to customer service, that's a signal something didn't go right. That signal costs money to acknowledge. It costs even more to resolve. If a human gets involved? That's a catastrophic loss on their internal actuarial table.

Think about it: You've already bought the product. You've already paid. The transaction is complete. The company's job, from a pure profit perspective, is done.

Everything that happens after that sale is just... expense.

Of course, smart companies understand that expense can be an investment in future sales, customer loyalty, and word-of-mouth marketing. But "future" and "maybe" don't show up well in quarterly financial reports.

So, companies optimize for the immediate reality: minimize the cost of dealing with you after they have your money.

The Insurance Company Playbook

The most profitable insurance companies in the world have figured something out:

If they make the claims process just annoying enough, just slow enough, just bureaucratic enough... some percentage of people will give up. They'll eat the loss. Move on.

Congratulations they just protected their margin.

The customer service playbook is no different.

Have you ever tried to cancel a subscription and ended up in a labyrinth of dark patterns, dropdown menus, and "are you sure you want to leave?" hostage negotiations? That's denial of coverage.

Have you ever sat through a chatbot loop so maddening you started doubting your own humanity? That's the digital version of a $500 deductible.

Have you ever waited 14 days for an email response that just said, "please refer to our FAQ"? That's the customer service equivalent of an insurance adjuster ghosting your calls.

I'm not being cynical. I'm just telling you the design.

The Attrition Strategy

Here's the number that will shock you: most companies measure something called "deflection rate." That's the percentage of customers who contact support but never reach a human.

In a sane world, companies would want that number to be low. They'd want customers to get help when they need it.

But in the actual world, deflection rate is a key performance indicator that executives want to see go up. The higher the better.

Why? Because every deflected customer is money saved.

The math is simple:

- Customer calls → costs money

- Customer gives up → costs nothing

- Customer solves problem themselves → costs nothing and looks like "self-service adoption"

Companies don't measure how many customers they help. They measure how many customers they avoid helping.

Deflection. Let that word settle in. It's a bureaucrat's synonym for "go away."

The Quarterly Trap

The tragedy is that many customer service leaders genuinely want to do better. But they're trapped in a system that measures them on cost reduction, not customer satisfaction.

Take Sarah from our San Francisco dinner. Three months after that conversation, she tried to make the case for investing in her vision of great service. She had data. She had pilot programs. She had customer testimonials.

Her CFO asked one question: "What's the payback period?"

"Eighteen months," she said.

"Our planning cycles are twelve months," he replied. "Can you get it to twelve?"

She couldn't. Not honestly.

Service transformation is slow. It requires sustained investment, cultural change, training, and new systems. Companies don't flip a switch and suddenly have great customer service.

But budget cycles are annual. Executive bonuses are tied to this year's performance. Stock prices move on quarterly earnings.

So, service investment gets delayed. Postponed. Tabled for "next year" when the budget is better.

Next year never comes.

The Competitive Delusion

Here's the lie that keeps the system intact: "Our competitors have bad service too, so customers will tolerate it."

And companies are right. Mostly.

Look at any industry with terrible customer service airlines, telecom, cable. Do customers revolt? Do they choose providers based on service quality?

Rarely.

We choose based on price, convenience, and product features. Service quality becomes a tiebreaker at best. And since most companies in most industries have comparably terrible service, it's never really a tiebreaker.

This creates a race to the bottom. Why should companies invest in service when their competitors aren't? Why be an expensive provider when customers aren't willing to pay extra for better treatment?

The market, it turns out, doesn't actually reward good service. At least not in ways that show up in quarterly reports.

The Hidden Costs They Ignore

But here's what those quarterly reports don't capture:

- The customer who quietly switches to a competitor and never tells you why.

- The prospect who researches your company, reads the reviews about your customer service, and chooses someone else.

- The employee who burns out from dealing with angry customers all day and quits, taking six months of training investment with them.

- The viral tweet that costs you millions in brand damage.

- The regulatory attention that comes when your service gets so bad that politicians start asking questions.

These costs are real. But they're not immediate. They don't show up in this quarter's budget. They're someone else's problem, some other department's responsibility.

The Revenue Protection Reality

The irony is that customer service, done right, isn't really a cost center. It's revenue protection.

All customer companies retain through good service is a customer they don't have to replace through expensive marketing. Every problem solved quickly is a crisis that doesn't have to be managed later. Every positive experience is word-of-mouth marketing that doesn't have to be bought.

But our accounting systems don't measure revenue protection. They measure revenue generation and cost reduction. Service falls into the latter category, which means it's always under pressure to do less with less.

Until someone has the courage to reframe the conversation to treat service as an investment in keeping the customers companies already have, the math will continue to favor customer suffering.

The System is Working as Designed

So, when you're on hold for 45 minutes, when the chatbot sends you in circles, when the rep reads from a script that doesn't address your problem remember this:

It's not broken. It's working exactly as designed.

Every second you wait is a spreadsheet decision. A conscious choice. Somewhere, a CFO looked at the cost of shaving 3 minutes off your hold time and said, "Nah."

That's not cruelty. That's math.

The question is: what would it take to change the math?

Section 2: The Budget Hierarchy

Understanding the profit motive is just the beginning. To see how these economic forces play out in real companies, you need to understand the corporate budget hierarchy and where customer service sits in the pecking order.

Spoiler alert: it's not pretty.

Messi Gets the Budget, the Goalie Gets the Blame

Let me introduce you to David. He runs the customer service department for a $4 billion tech company. He's smart, empathetic, has a Wall Street Journal subscription and a Peloton. He genuinely cares about customers and has the data to prove that better service drives retention.

He's also invisible at his own executive table.

I watched him once during a board meeting where the marketing chief got a standing ovation for a rebrand that cost $11 million and delivered no new customers. The logo was sleeker. The colors were more "on-brand." The executives nodded approvingly at the deck full of awards from design agencies.

Twenty minutes later, David asked for half a million to improve service response time by 40%. He had pilot data. Customer testimonials. Retention projections.

He got told to "do more with less."

That's the pecking order.

Marketing is Messi. Everyone cheers when they score. Sales is Ronaldo flashy, expensive, but they bring in revenue. Product development is the midfield essential for moving the ball forward.

Customer service is the goalie. Make a save? Just relief. Miss once? Rage.

The Dopamine Gap

Here's why this hierarchy exists: service doesn't trigger the corporate brain's dopamine loop.

Nobody hugs a company because they finally got their refund processed. There's no parade for an accurate billing correction. Service is the thing you notice only when it fails and so companies invest just enough to make sure the wheels wobble, but don't fall off.

Which is why, when you go to the company website and click "Sales"? You're answered in 12 seconds. Click "Support"? Bring a sleeping bag.

The sales team gets the latest CRM technology, the best leads, the highest commissions, and first-class travel to conferences. The marketing team gets creative agencies, Super Bowl ads, and unlimited coffee from the fancy machine.

The customer service team gets last year's computers, a closet they call an office, and a Keurig with only hazelnut pods left.

The Investment Philosophy

This isn't random. There's a logic to it, twisted, but logical.

Corporate investment follows a simple principle: fund what grows, starve what doesn't.

Sales grows revenue directly. Marketing grows awareness and pipeline. Product development creates new revenue streams. These departments are seen as profit centers.

Customer service, in the corporate mind, prevents revenue loss. It's damage control. It's expense management. It's a cost center.

And cost centers get cost center treatment: minimize spending, maximize efficiency, optimize for cheap.

The Budget Meeting Reality

I've sat in on hundreds of budget planning meetings across dozens of companies. Here's how the conversation always goes:

Sales: "We need $50 million for headcount expansion. We can grow revenue 30%."
 Everyone: "Approved!"

Marketing: "We need $30 million for the brand campaign. We'll increase market awareness by 15%."

 Everyone: "Love it!"

Product: "We need $20 million for R&D. We're building the future."

 Everyone: "Visionary!"

Customer Service: "We need $2 million to reduce hold times and hire enough staff to "

 Everyone: "What's the Return on Investment on that?"

Every. Single. Time.

Service has to justify every dollar with mathematical precision while other departments get approved on aspirational PowerPoints and hockey stick growth projections.

The Measurement Problem

Here's why customer service can never win the budget game: it's measured differently than every other department.

Sales gets measured on revenue growth. Bigger numbers = bigger budgets next year.

Marketing gets measured on lead generation, brand awareness, customer acquisition. All forward-looking metrics tied to growth.

Product gets measured on feature delivery, user adoption, market differentiation. Innovation metrics that suggest future success.

Customer Service gets measured on cost per contact, average handle time, and containment rates. Every metric is about doing less, spending less, touching customers less.

Companies can't win a growth game with shrinkage metrics.

The Sarah Dilemma

Remember Sarah from our San Francisco dinner? Three months after that conversation, she built a bulletproof business case for service investment.

She proved that customers who had positive service experiences spent 23% more in the following year. She showed that reducing hold times from 8 minutes to 3 minutes would increase customer lifetime value by $340 per customer. She calculated that better service would reduce churn (customers leaving) by 15%, saving $4.1 million in replacement acquisition costs.

The math was ironclad. The presentation was flawless.

Her CFO asked one question: "What's the payback period?"

"Eighteen months," she said.

"Our planning cycles are twelve months," he replied. "Can you get it to twelve?"

She couldn't. Not honestly.

And there's the trap: service transformation takes time. Companies don't flip a switch and suddenly have amazing customer experience. They need to hire people, train them, change systems, and shift culture. It's a marathon, not a sprint.

But budget cycles are annual. Executive bonuses are tied to this year's performance. Stock prices move on quarterly earnings. The CFO isn't being unreasonable; he's being realistic about how his own performance gets measured.

The Quarterly Earnings Call

Want to know why service investment gets killed? Listen to a quarterly earnings call.

Analysts ask about revenue growth, margin expansion, market share gains, product launches. They want to know about the competitive landscape, the sales pipeline, the marketing strategy.

Nobody asks about customer service. Nobody inquires about support quality. No analyst has ever said, "Tell me about your hold times and how they're affecting customer satisfaction."

Because service doesn't move stock prices. At least not in ways that show up in quarterly reports.

The CEO who announces, "We're investing $10 million in better customer service" will get questions about margin compression and cost discipline.

The CEO who announces, "We're cutting customer service costs by $10 million through automation" will get praise for operational excellence.

The incentives are perfectly clear.

The Consultant's Confession

I need to admit something here: I was part of the problem.

For years, I sold "customer experience optimization" projects that were really just cost reduction exercises in disguise. The language was about "improving efficiency" and "streamlining the customer journey," but the goal was always the same: handle more customers with fewer people.

I helped companies implement chatbots not because they improved customer satisfaction (they usually didn't), but because they deflected volume from expensive human agents. I designed IVR systems not to help customers navigate faster, but to filter out "low-value" calls before they reached humans.

The clients loved it because I could show immediate cost savings. The customers hated it because the experience got worse. But customers don't write the checks.

I kept telling myself that better efficiency would eventually lead to better experiences. That if we could handle simple issues with automation, humans could focus on complex problems.

But that's not what happened. Companies just used automation to handle the same volume with fewer humans. The complex problems still went to understaffed, overwhelmed agents who now had even less time per customer.

The Innovation Theater

Here's the cruelest irony: companies love to talk about "innovative customer experience" while systematically underfunding the department responsible for delivering it.

They'll spend millions on customer journey mapping exercises, design thinking workshops, and CX transformation consultants. They'll create beautiful customer experience vision statements and hang them in the break room.

But when it comes to actually funding better service, hiring more agents, improving training, upgrading systems, suddenly it's "let's see what we can do with existing resources."

It's innovation theater. All the performance of caring about customers without the budget to actually care.

The Private Equity Playbook

The budget hierarchy gets even more brutal when private equity gets involved. I've worked with dozens of PE-backed companies, and the playbook is always the same:

Month 1: "Customer experience is our top priority."

Month 6: "We need to optimize customer service costs."

Month 12: "Let's explore offshore options."

Month 18: "AI should handle most of these interactions."

Month 24: "We've successfully streamlined customer operations."

Translation: they fired half the customer service team, outsourced the rest to the Philippines, and replaced human interactions with chatbots wherever possible.

The numbers look great on the P&L. Customer satisfaction plummets, but that's a problem for the next owner.

The Acquisition Trap

The budget hierarchy also explains why service quality often deteriorates after acquisitions.

When Company A buys Company B, the first thing they look at is "operational synergies" MBA speak for "what can we cut?"

Customer service is always the low-hanging fruit. Why maintain two call centers when companies can route all calls to one? Why keep both sets of service reps when the "best practices" from Company A can be applied everywhere?

I watched a tech company acquire a smaller competitor specifically because they loved their customer service culture. Six months later, they had "integrated" the acquisition by laying off the entire customer service team and routing calls to their existing center in India.

The acquiring executives genuinely didn't understand why customer satisfaction scores dropped after the "integration." They had kept the same service levels (12-hour email response time) and the same scripts. What was the problem?

The problem was that they had kept the service structure but killed the service culture. And culture can't be integrated on a spreadsheet.

The Growth Stage Trap

Startup companies often begin with amazing customer service. When they have 100 customers, the founder can personally respond to every support email. When they have 1,000 customers, they can hire one great person who knows everyone's name.

But when they scale to 10,000 customers? 100,000? The math changes.

I watched a SaaS startup grow from $1 million to $50 million in revenue over three years. In year one, their NPS was 87. Customers loved them. The founder still answered support emails personally.

By year three, their NPS was 34. What happened?

Nothing dramatic. Just the gradual application of "business discipline" to customer service:

- They hired cheaper, less experienced agents

- They implemented productivity metrics (calls per hour, average handle time)

- They added automated responses and chatbots

- They moved from email to a ticketing system

- They outsourced overnight support to save costs

- They started measuring deflection rates

Each change made sense individually. Each change saved money. Each change made the experience slightly worse.

Death by a thousand cuts.

The Venture Capital Pressure

The startup customer service death spiral gets worse when VCs get involved. I've been in board meetings where customer service comes up exactly once: when discussing the path to profitability.

"What's your customer acquisition cost versus lifetime value ratio?"
"How do we optimize unit economics?"
"When do you hit positive unit economics?"
"What's the plan for scaling operational efficiency?"

Notice what's missing? Any discussion of customer satisfaction, service quality, or long-term brand building.

VCs are optimizing for 10x returns over 5-7 years. Customer service is seen as a drag on those returns pure cost with unclear benefits.

The portfolio company CEOs know this. So they optimize for the metrics that matter to their investors: growth rate, unit economics, path to profitability.

Customer happiness isn't in that list.

The Public Company Pressure Cooker

If VC pressure is bad, public company pressure is worse.

Every 90 days, companies have to stand in front of analysts and explain why their margins aren't expanding faster. Every quarter, investors expect operating leverage more revenue with proportionally less cost.

Customer service is the easiest place to find that leverage. Companies can automate it, outsource it, deflect it. The cost savings show up immediately in quarterly reports.

The customer satisfaction damage shows up later in churn rates, acquisition costs, brand perception. But later is someone else's problem.

I consulted a public company CEO who told me, "I'd love to invest in better service, but Wall Street punishes companies that sacrifice short-term margins for long-term customer relationships."

He wasn't wrong. Companies that announce major service investments often see their stock price drop as analysts worry about margin compression.

Companies that announce service automation and cost reduction often see their stock price rise as analysts applaud operational efficiency.

The Executive Bonus Structure

Want to know why customer service stays underfunded? Look at how executives get paid.

CEOs get bonuses tied to revenue growth, margin expansion, and stock price performance.

CFOs get bonuses tied to cost management, operational efficiency, and hitting financial targets.

The Head of Sales gets bonuses tied to revenue generation and pipeline development.

The Head of Marketing gets bonuses tied to lead generation and brand metrics.

The Head of Customer Service gets bonuses tied to... cost per contact and containment rates.

See the problem?

Everyone else gets rewarded for growth. The customer service leader gets rewarded for spending less money and handling fewer interactions.

Companies get what they incentivize. And the incentives are crystal clear: customer service is about cost minimization, not customer satisfaction.

The Breaking Point

This system would collapse if customers actually punished bad service by switching providers. But in most industries, they don't.

Airlines all have terrible service, so customers choose based on price and routes.

Cable companies all have terrible service, so customers choose based on speed and bundling.

Banks all have terrible service, so customers choose based on fees and convenience.

As long as terrible service is universally terrible, no individual company pays a meaningful price for being part of the problem.

The budget hierarchy persists because the market allows it to persist.

The Rare Exception

Occasionally, you find a company that breaks the hierarchy. Usually, it's because the founder or CEO has personally experienced customer service hell and refuses to perpetuate it.

I worked with a CEO who had spent three days trying to get a simple billing issue resolved with his previous company's phone provider. Three days of transfers, hold times, and scripted non-answers.

When he started his own company, his first hire was a head of customer success not customer service, customer success. The budget for that department was 15% of revenue. The team reported directly to him.

His investors thought he was crazy. "You're spending way too much on customer success. You need to optimize those unit economics."

Five years later, his customer acquisition cost was 60% lower than industry average because of word-of-mouth referrals. His churn rate was 40% lower because customers actually liked dealing with the company.

His investors stopped complaining about the customer success budget.

But this CEO was an exception. Most executives are trapped in the budget hierarchy, optimizing for metrics that reward cutting service, not improving it.

The Cultural Trickle-Down

The budget hierarchy doesn't just affect resource allocation. It shapes company culture.

When customer service is consistently underfunded relative to other departments, it sends a message: this work is less important. These people are less valuable. These problems are lower priority.

That message trickles down through the entire organization.

Product teams build features without considering service implications.

Marketing teams make promises that service can't keep.

Sales teams sell packages that the service doesn't know how to support.

Executive teams celebrate revenue milestones but ignore service failures.

The customer service team becomes the organizational equivalent of the janitor necessary but invisible, appreciated only when something goes really wrong.

Tomorrow's Crisis, Today's Budget

Here's the final irony: companies that starve customer service today will spend multiples fixing the problems tomorrow.

A crisis management firm charges $50,000 per day when service failures go viral.

A class-action lawsuit settlement costs millions when service practices cross legal lines.

Rebuilding brand reputation after a service disaster costs tens of millions.

But those costs show up in different fiscal years, different budget categories, different departments' P&Ls.

The CFO who cut customer service costs by $5 million this year will be long gone when the company spends $50 million on crisis management three years from now.

The Solution Hidden in Plain Sight

The budget hierarchy could be fixed with a simple accounting change: measure customer service as revenue protection, not cost generation.

Instead of tracking cost per contact, track revenue retained per contact.

Instead of measuring deflection rates, measure customer lifetime value by service tier.

Instead of optimizing for cheap, optimize for profitable relationships.

But that would require admitting that the current system is designed to create the problems it's supposed to solve.

And admitting that would mean changing a lot more than just the customer service budget.

It would mean changing how we think about customers, how we measure success, and how we define value in the modern economy.

Which brings us to the next part of our economic story: how technology became the ultimate tool for avoiding customers while claiming to serve them better.

Section 3: The Technology Smokescreen

Now we get to the part where companies pretend to solve their customer service problems without actually spending money on customer service.

Welcome to the technology smokescreen where every customer interaction becomes an opportunity to avoid human contact, and every dollar saved on people gets rebranded as "digital transformation."

The Great Deflection

Let me re-introduce you to my favorite customer service metric. It's called "deflection rate" the percentage of customers who contact support but never reach a human.

In a sane world, companies would want that number to be low. They'd want customers to get help when they need it.

But in the actual world, deflection rate is a key performance indicator that executives want to see go up. The higher the better.

I once consulted for a telecom company whose VP of Operations proudly told me they had achieved a 73% deflection rate. Seventy-three percent of customers who called for help never spoke to a human being.

"That's terrible," I said.

"That's efficient," he replied.

The math was simple in his mind:

- Customer reaches human → costs $6.50 per interaction

- Customer deflected by automation → costs $0.47 per interaction

- Customer gives up → costs $0.00 per interaction

Guess which outcome the system was optimized for?

Digital Dodgeball

Companies don't call it deflection in their marketing materials. They call it "self-service" and "customer empowerment" and "omnichannel optimization."

But I call it what it is: digital dodgeball.

The goal isn't to help you. The goal is to avoid you. Every piece of technology, every chatbot, every FAQ page, every phone tree menu is designed with one primary objective: keep you away from expensive humans.

Take the modern phone tree. When I started in customer service, these systems had maybe 4-5 options. Press 1 for billing, press 2 for technical support, press 3 for new sales.

Now? I've audited phone trees with 47 different menu options spread across seven layers of submenus. You can press numbers for 12 minutes before the system even considers connecting you to a human.

And if you try to outsmart the system by pressing "0" or saying "representative"? Many companies have programmed their systems to ignore those commands entirely. You get a polite voice saying, "I didn't understand that. Let me help you find what you're looking for."

Translation: "I understood perfectly. I'm just not going to let you escape."

The IVR Hall of Fame

I once called an IVR system that handled 24 million calls a year. Twenty-four million frustrated customers navigating a labyrinth designed by committee and implemented by people who had never used it.

It was awful. Truly, catastrophically awful.

The executive who ran it bragged to me about saving $50 million annually.

"Do you want to make it better?" I asked.

He looked confused. "Why? The system works."

And there it was. The perfect summary of modern customer service technology: it works perfectly for the company. The fact that it tortures customers is not a bug, it's a feature.

That executive wasn't evil. He wasn't cruel. He was doing exactly what his performance metrics told him to do: minimize cost per contact while maintaining "service availability."

The system was available. You could call it 24/7. Whether you could actually get help was a different question entirely.

The Chatbot Revolution That Wasn't

If phone trees are bad, chatbots are worse. Because at least with a phone tree, you know you're dealing with a machine.

Chatbots pretend to be helpful while being fundamentally useless for anything beyond the simplest transactions.

"Hi! I'm Mary, your virtual assistant! How can I help you today? 😊"

Mary isn't a person. Mary is a decision tree wrapped in emoji and false empathy. Mary has exactly 37 pre-written responses and will route 73% of conversations into dead ends.

But Mary saves the company money, so Mary is everywhere.

I helped build some of the early chatbot systems in the 2000s. The promise was beautiful: artificial intelligence that could understand natural language, learn from interactions, and provide personalized help 24/7.

The reality? Most chatbots today are barely more sophisticated than the ELIZA program from 1966, a simple pattern-matching system that reflects your questions back as statements.

You: "My order is late."
 Bot: "I understand you're concerned about your order. Let me help you track that!"

You: "Where is it?"

Bot: "I'd be happy to help you with tracking information! Can you provide your order number?"

You: "I already did."

Bot: "I apologize for any confusion. For the best assistance with order tracking, I recommend visiting our help center or speaking with a specialist."

Translation: "I have no idea what you're talking about, but I've successfully wasted 3 minutes of your time while sounding helpful."

The AI Delusion

But wait, it gets worse. Now we have "AI-powered customer service" that promises to revolutionize everything. Matthew McConaughey is on every other commercial hawking 'Agentforce' the AI solution from Salesforce.

Executives everywhere are foaming at the mouth, dreaming of a world where no one has to talk to a customer ever again:

- Customers will love talking to bots

- Bots will resolve most issues without human help

- AI will personalize everything like magic

- Support costs will drop like a rock

- NPS will soar, retention will spike, margins will expand

I've sat through hundreds of sales presentations promising this AI utopia. The vendors always show the same demo: a customer with a simple question gets a perfect answer in 30 seconds from an AI that somehow knows their entire history and anticipates their needs.

What they don't show you: the 75% of interactions where the AI fails spectacularly and the customer ends up more frustrated than when they started.

The Real AI Numbers

Here's what actually happens when companies deploy "AI-powered customer service":

- 75% of chatbot interactions still require human handoff

- Customer satisfaction scores drop by 23% on average

- Average resolution time increases by 40% (because customers waste time with bots first)

- Employee satisfaction drops as agents have to clean up AI failures

- Actual cost savings: 12% (far less than projected)

But the AI vendors have learned to game the metrics. They measure "automation rate" (how many interactions start with AI) rather than "resolution rate" (how many interactions are actually resolved by AI).

They measure "containment" (how many customers give up) rather than "satisfaction" (how many customers get their problems solved).

They measure "efficiency" (cost per interaction) rather than "effectiveness" (problems actually resolved).

It's measurement theater designed to hide the fact that the technology doesn't work for customers, it only works for budgets.

The Outsourcing Double-Whammy

Just when you think it can't get worse, companies discovered they could combine technology avoidance with geographic arbitrage.

First, they implement systems to deflect as many customers as possible away from humans. Then, for the customers who manage to fight through the digital maze, they route them to the cheapest humans available usually on the other side of the world.

I've flown to Bogotá, Manila, Mumbai, and Krakow, all in search of cheaper labor for American customer service operations. Beautiful places that only made sense to the CFO.

The pitch is always the same: "Same quality service at 60% lower cost!"

The reality is never the same. Cultural nuances get lost. Accents create communication barriers. Time zones complicate escalations. And most importantly, the offshore teams have even less authority to solve problems than their domestic counterparts.

But the spreadsheet math works: $15/hour in Oklahoma becomes $4/hour in the Philippines. The customer experience suffers, but the quarterly budget improves.

The Self-Service Trap

The latest evolution of the technology smokescreen is "customer empowerment through self-service."

Companies love this language because it makes customers doing all the work sound like a benefit. "We're empowering you to solve your own problems!"

And to be fair, good self-service can be genuinely helpful. I want to check my bank balance at 2 AM without talking to anyone. I want to track my package without calling UPS.

But bad self-service is just another deflection tactic wrapped in empowerment rhetoric.

Ever tried to cancel a subscription online? The sign-up process is one click, but cancellation requires navigating through 47 screens of retention offers and dark patterns designed to make you give up.

Ever tried to dispute a charge through a bank's website? You fill out forms that ask for information the bank already has, upload documents that disappear into digital void, and wait for responses that may or may not come.

The self-service isn't empowering you, it's conscripting you into doing the bank's work for free.

The Help Center Mirage

Every company now has a "Help Center" or "Knowledge Base" filled with articles that sound helpful but rarely address your actual problem.

Search for "how to cancel my subscription" and you get articles about "managing your account preferences" and "updating billing information" and "temporarily pausing service" everything except actually canceling.

These help centers aren't designed to help. They're designed to exhaust you. The theory is that if you spend 20 minutes reading unhelpful articles, you might solve your problem yourself, give up entirely, or at least be too tired to complain when you finally reach a human.

I've written some of these articles. The internal guidance was always the same: "Be helpful enough that customers feel like we care, but not so helpful that they actually get what they want without talking to retention."

The Omnichannel Shell Game

Another hot buzzword in customer service technology is "omnichannel" , the promise that you can start a conversation on chat, continue it via email, and finish it on the phone, with perfect continuity throughout.

In reality, omnichannel usually means you get to repeat your problem on multiple channels while different systems fail to talk to each other.

You start a chat. The bot can't help. You get transferred to email support. They can't see your chat history. You call the phone number. They can't access your email ticket. You go to social media. They ask you to DM your account details.

Same problem, four channels, zero resolution.

But the company gets to say they offer "seamless omnichannel support" while actually providing a more fragmented experience than if they just had one working phone number.

The Metrics Theater

All of this technology gets justified through careful measurement of the wrong things.

Companies measure:

- Automation rate (how many interactions start with bots)

- Deflection rate (how many customers never reach humans)

- Cost per contact (how little they spend per interaction)

- Average handle time (how quickly they get rid of customers)

They don't measure:

- Problem resolution rate (how many issues actually get solved)

- Customer effort score (how hard it is to get help)

- Emotional outcome (how customers feel after the interaction)

- Long-term relationship impact (how service affects loyalty)

It's measurement theater designed to justify technology investments that make the experience worse while making the budget better.

The Executive Echo Chamber

The people making these technology decisions rarely experience their own customer service.

They have executive assistants who handle their personal customer service issues. They have corporate accounts with dedicated relationship managers. They get whisked past the normal customer experience straight to VIP treatment.

I once asked a CEO to call his own customer service line. He couldn't find the phone number on the website. When he finally called, he hung up after 12 minutes on hold.

"Is this what our customers go through?" he asked.

"Every day," I said.

"We need to fix this," he said.

Three months later, his company launched a new chatbot initiative to "optimize the customer journey through AI-powered automation."

Nothing was fixed. More technology was just layered on top of the broken foundation.

The Vendor Ecosystem

There's an entire industry built around selling technology solutions to customer service problems that could be solved by hiring more humans and giving them authority to help.

Customer service technology conferences are surreal experiences. Vendor after vendor promising to "revolutionize customer experience" with AI, automation, analytics, and integration platforms.

None of them mention hiring better people or training them properly or empowering them to solve problems. That's not scalable. That's not disruptive. That's not a technology solution.

But that's usually what actually works.

The COVID Acceleration

The pandemic accelerated every bad trend in customer service technology. Companies had legitimate reasons to reduce human contact, but they used the crisis as cover for changes they wanted to make anyway.

"Due to COVID-19, we're experiencing higher than normal call volumes. Please visit our website for faster service."

That message is still playing in 2025, five years after the pandemic ended.

COVID became the excuse for permanent degradation of human service, wrapped in public health language but motivated by cost reduction.

The Breaking Point

Here's what the technology vendors never tell you: every automated system has a breaking point. A complexity threshold beyond which humans are not just better, but essential.

Your chatbot can handle "What are your hours?" It cannot handle "My husband died and I need to remove him from our joint account but I don't have his death certificate yet and our mortgage payment is due tomorrow."

Your IVR can route simple billing questions. It cannot handle "My disabled daughter was charged for services she can't use and your app isn't accessible and I've been trying to resolve this for two months."

Your help center can explain basic features. It cannot navigate the emotional complexity of a customer who feels betrayed by a company they trusted.

But companies keep pushing more interactions toward automation, regardless of complexity, because the cost savings are immediate and the customer frustration is someone else's problem.

The Real Innovation

The most successful implementations are the ones you never notice.

The credit card company that uses AI to detect fraud before it affects you.

The airline that automatically rebooks you on a better flight before your original flight gets delayed.

The bank that identifies billing errors and fixes them before you see them on your statement.

The streaming service that detects buffering issues and adjusts video quality in real-time.

Good customer service technology works behind the scenes to prevent problems, not to avoid customers who have problems.

But prevention doesn't create obvious cost savings. It doesn't generate impressive deflection metrics. It doesn't produce dramatic automation rates.

So companies keep investing in technology that avoids customers rather than technology that serves them.

The Way Forward

The technology smokescreen could be lifted with a simple shift in perspective: use technology to make humans better, not to replace humans entirely.

AI that gives customer service reps complete context before a call starts.

Automation that handles simple transactions so humans can focus on complex problems.

Analytics that identify systemic issues so they can be fixed at the source.

Integration that eliminates customer effort rather than company cost.

But that would require admitting that the goal should be better service, not cheaper service.

And admitting that would mean changing the fundamental economics that created the smokescreen in the first place.

Which brings us to the human cost of all this technological "efficiency" and why the people on the front lines of customer service may be suffering even more than the customers they're trying to help.

Section 4: The Human Cost

We've talked about the profit motive, the budget hierarchy, and the technology smokescreen. Now let's talk about the people caught in the middle: the customer service representatives who have to deliver on promises their companies never intended to keep, using tools designed to frustrate customers and metrics that punish empathy.

If you think calling customer service is hell, try working in it.

Welcome to the Panopticon

Federal prisoners have more freedom than most contact center reps.

Agents get a schedule. Not a flexible one. A militarized one. Clock in at 8:00:00 AM, not 8:00:01. Lunch break from 12:15 to 1:00 PM. Bathroom breaks tracked to the minute. Clock out at exactly 5:00 PM after the computer confirms all required tasks are completed.

Bathroom breaks? Tracked and timed. In some centers I've audited, agents need supervisor approval for breaks longer than 4 minutes. I've seen weekly reports that included metrics like "average restroom duration per agent."

Every call? Recorded and scored by algorithms that measure tone, word choice, script adherence, and dead air time.

Every word? Monitored for compliance with a script written by lawyers and consultants who have never spoken to an angry customer.

Back when I ran a center, I'd sit with reps and review weekly reports that included how long they spent in the bathroom. I wish I was joking. One report showed that Jennifer in Customer Care had "exceeded optimal break time by 23 minutes this week."

Jennifer was dealing with a stomach bug. She didn't feel comfortable sharing that with her supervisor. So it went in her file as "time management issue."

The Impossible Metrics

Customer service reps are measured on contradictory goals that make success mathematically impossible.

Speed vs. Quality: Handle calls quickly (average target: 6 minutes) but solve every problem completely. Rush through interactions but make customers feel heard and valued.

Script Adherence vs. Problem Solving: Follow the exact script that legal approved, but adapt to each customer's unique situation. Sound natural while reading predetermined responses.

Cost Control vs. Customer Satisfaction: Don't give away money in credits or refunds, but make angry customers happy. Say no to requests while maintaining positive sentiment scores.

Productivity vs. Accuracy: Take as many calls as possible per hour, but don't make mistakes that require callbacks or escalations.

I once reviewed performance metrics for a cable company where the top-performing agent by productivity score (most calls handled per hour) had the lowest customer satisfaction rating. The highest customer satisfaction scores belonged to an agent who was written up monthly for "failing to meet productivity targets."

The system literally punished the behavior it claimed to want.

The Authority Vacuum

Here's the cruelest part: even when customer service reps want to help, they can't.

They're given titles like "Customer Care Specialist" and "Service Representative," but they have less authority than a McDonald's shift manager. At least the shift manager can comp a burger.

I audited a credit card company where agents needed supervisor approval for credits above $25. Twenty-five dollars. For a company that charges $39 annual fees and $35 late fees.

Picture this scenario:

- Customer calls about a legitimate billing error for $47

- Agent can see it's clearly an error in the system

- Customer has been a cardholder for 8 years with perfect payment history

- The fix requires a $47 credit

Should take 2 minutes. Instead:

- Agent explains she needs supervisor approval (customer gets annoyed)

- Customer placed on hold while agent searches for available supervisor

- All supervisors busy with other "approvals"

- Customer waits 18 minutes on hold

- Supervisor finally available, reviews obvious error

- Supervisor approves obvious credit

- Agent processes credit and apologizes for delay

Total call time: 23 minutes. Cost to company: $14.50 in agent time plus $8.25 in supervisor time. Customer satisfaction: destroyed.

All to approve a credit that any reasonable person would issue immediately.

But the policy exists because some consultant calculated that requiring approval for credits above $25 would "reduce unauthorized credits by 15%."

Nobody calculated the cost of 23-minute calls instead of 2-minute calls. Nobody measured the customer frustration. Nobody tracked the agent burnout from apologizing for policies they didn't create and can't change.

The Garbage Tools Problem

Companies love to say "Our service reps are our most important people." But they don't show it.

They hand agents garbage tools systems that don't talk to each other, screens layered ten-deep, software that crashes when you need it most. Then they wonder why customers don't get help.

I've watched agents navigate through 8 different systems to answer a single billing question:

1. Customer management system (to verify identity)

2. Billing system (to see charges)

3. Payment processing system (to see payment history)

4. Product catalog system (to understand what was purchased)

5. Promotional system (to see active discounts)

6. Trouble ticket system (to check previous complaints)

7. Knowledge base system (to find resolution procedures)

8. Authorization system (to get approval for any changes)

Each system has different login requirements. Each loads slowly. None of them communicate with the others. The customer waits while the agent clicks through digital purgatory, apologizing every 30 seconds for the delay.

When the systems inevitably fail (usually during peak call volume), agents fall back to paper procedures and manual workarounds that make everything take three times longer.

But instead of fixing the technology, companies add a second monitor.

They don't raise pay. They don't fix the systems. They don't ease the policies. They just give agents two monitors to stare at while they get screamed at by people with broken routers.

The Script Prison

Most customer service training doesn't teach problem-solving. It teaches performance art.

New reps don't go to training, they go to reprogramming. Scripted greetings. "Soft skills" scorecards. Empathy modules that teach them to fake caring without actually caring.

The scripts are written by committees of lawyers and brand consultants who have never taken an angry customer call. Every word is focus-grouped and legal-approved and completely unnatural.

"Thank you for calling [Company Name], where customer satisfaction is our top priority. My name is Jennifer and I'll be happy to assist you today. May I please have your account number so I can better serve you?"

No human talks like that. But if Jennifer deviates from the script if she says "Hi, this is Jennifer, how can I help you?" she gets marked down for "failing to follow brand guidelines."

The result is that calling customer service feels like talking to robots pretending to be human. You hear phrases like:

- "I do apologize for the inconvenience"

- "Thank you for being a valued customer"

- "I see you've been with us for 10 years. Great job!"

- "Is there anything else I can help you with today?"

It's not just awkward. It's fake. Weaponized politeness designed to sound caring while actually providing no care at all.

The Emotional Labor Tax

Customer service work is exhausting in ways that don't show up in job descriptions.

Agents absorb anger all day from people who aren't really angry at them; they're angry at the system, the policies, the company. But agents are the face of all of it. They're the lightning rod for frustration that's been building through 20 minutes of hold time and 3 failed chatbot interactions.

I've sat with agents who dealt with:

- A man screaming about his cancer treatment being denied by insurance

- A woman crying because her dead husband's phone line couldn't be canceled without death certificates she didn't have

- A small business owner facing bankruptcy because a payment processing error froze his merchant account

- A college student whose financial aid was delayed, jeopardizing her enrollment

These agents wanted to help. They empathized with the pain. But they were equipped with scripts that said "I understand your frustration" and policies that prevented them from doing anything meaningful about it.

The emotional toll is real. Turnover in customer service centers averages 75% annually. In bad centers, it can hit 150% meaning they replace every position more than once per year.

The Surveillance State

Modern customer service work is surveillance capitalism applied to human empathy.

Every call is recorded and analyzed for "quality assurance." But quality assurance really means compliance monitoring. Did agents say the words in the right order? Did they hit all the required script points? Did they avoid saying anything that could create legal liability?

It doesn't measure whether they actually helped the customer. It measures whether they performed help convincingly.

I worked with one company whose "quality score" algorithm flagged an agent for saying "That's ridiculous" when a customer described a clearly absurd billing error. The agent was empathizing with the customer's frustration and agreeing that the error was unreasonable.

But the system flagged "ridiculous" as "negative language" and docked the agent's quality score. Her supervisor had to coach her to say "I understand why that would be frustrating" instead.

Same sentiment. More words. Less human. Higher score.

The Impossible Empathy

Companies want customer service reps to be empathetic, but only in ways that don't cost money.

Express understanding, but don't offer solutions the company doesn't approve.

Show that you care, but don't care so much that you bend rules.

Be human, but follow inhuman policies.

Sound genuine while reading from a script.

I once sat in on a training session where new hires were taught "empathy techniques":

- "Mirror the customer's language"

- "Use emotional labeling: 'That sounds frustrating'"

- "Validate their feelings: 'I would feel the same way'"

- "Transition to solutions: 'Let me see what I can do'"

It was empathy as performance technique. Caring as a customer service theater.

The trainer never mentioned actually feeling empathy for customers. It was all about performing empathy convincingly enough to improve satisfaction scores.

The Breaking Point Stories

I've collected hundreds of stories from customer service workers who reached their breaking point. Here are three that haunt me:

Shannon, Insurance Claims: "A woman called because her daughter's insulin prescription was denied. She was crying, saying she couldn't afford to pay out of pocket and didn't know what to do. I spent 45 minutes on the phone, found the error in our system, and fixed it. My supervisor wrote me up for 'excessive call time' and said I should have transferred her to the pharmacy benefits line after 10 minutes."

Marcus, Cable Company: "An elderly man called because his internet was out and he couldn't video call his grandchildren. His son had set it up for him before deploying overseas. I wanted to walk him through the setup, but our policy is to charge $89 for 'technical support' beyond basic troubleshooting. I was supposed to sell him the service call. He couldn't afford it. I stayed late and called him back after my shift to help for free. If my manager found out, I'd be fired."

Jennifer, Telecom: "A small business owner called because a billing error had caused his phone lines to be shut off during his busiest season. He was losing thousands of dollars per day. I could see the error in our system as a simple coding mistake but I needed three different approvals to fix it. The process would take 'up to 5 business days.' He was sobbing on the phone. I've never felt more useless in my life."

The Good Rep Punishment

The cruelest irony is that the best customer service reps the ones who actually care about helping people get punished by the system.

They spend extra time making sure problems are really solved, which hurts their productivity metrics.

They escalate issues that need escalation, which gets them labeled as "high escalation rate" problems.

They advocate for customers against unfair policies, which gets them coached on "company loyalty."

They form emotional connections with customers, which makes the emotional labor even more exhausting.

Meanwhile, the reps who master the system who can rush through calls, stick to scripts, deflect escalations, and sound helpful while providing no actual help get promoted to supervisor roles where they train the next generation to game the system.

The system rewards performance of service over delivery of service.

The Outsourcing Double Punishment

When companies outsource customer service, they create an additional layer of worker exploitation.

The offshore agents often have better education and language skills than their domestic counterparts. I've worked with customer service reps in the

Philippines who have engineering degrees and speak three languages fluently.

But they're paid $3-4 per hour to absorb anger from American customers who are frustrated with American companies about American policies that the offshore agents have no power to change.

They get yelled at for decisions made in boardrooms they'll never see by executives they'll never meet about policies they had no role in creating.

And they can't even fight back. Their job depends on maintaining "professional demeanor" no matter how badly they're treated.

I've listened to calls where customers berated offshore agents with racist language, questioned their intelligence, and demanded to speak to "someone in America." The agents are trained to absorb it all with scripted apologies.

The Dignity Deficit

At its core, modern customer service work is designed to strip away human dignity from both customers and workers.

Customers are reduced to numbers, metrics, and data points.

Workers are reduced to voices reading scripts, hands inputting data, and bodies occupying workstations.

The human connection that should be at the heart of service, one person helping another person solve a problem gets optimized away in favor of efficiency metrics and cost control.

The Quiet Rebellion

Despite all this, I've met customer service workers who find ways to maintain their humanity within an inhuman system.

The agent who "forgets" to mention the $25 fee when helping a customer who clearly can't afford it.

The supervisor who approves credits without the required documentation when the situation warrants it.

The rep who spends her own break time following up on complex cases to make sure they're resolved.

The team lead who shields her agents from unreasonable policies when possible.

These acts of quiet rebellion keep the system from being completely heartless. But they shouldn't be necessary.

Workers shouldn't have to risk their jobs to provide basic human decency.

The Resignation Phase

Most customer service workers go through predictable phases:

Month 1-3: Optimism - "I'm going to help people and make a difference"

Month 4-8: Frustration - "Why is this system so hard to work with?"

Month 9-12: Anger - "These policies are designed to hurt customers"

Month 13+: Resignation - "I'll do my job, collect my paycheck, and try not to care"

The workers who survive long-term are usually the ones who learn to emotionally disconnect. They perform empathy without feeling it. They follow scripts without thinking about their impact. They clock in, handle their calls, and clock out.

The system breaks their spirit as surely as it breaks customer trust.

The Staffing Death Spiral

The human cost creates a vicious cycle:

Bad working conditions → High turnover → Constant training of new, inexperienced agents → Worse customer experiences → More angry customers → Worse working conditions → Higher turnover

Companies respond to high turnover by making jobs easier to fill rather than better to keep. They dumb down requirements, simplify training, and create more restrictive policies to limit the damage that undertrained agents can do.

This creates a death spiral where the job becomes progressively less skilled, less empowering, and less human.

The Breaking Point

Over 50% increase in violence against retail customer service workers in recent years. Customers are angrier. Workers are more vulnerable. The social contract of civil interaction is breaking down.

I can't call 1-800 numbers in front of young children anymore. Not because of explicit content, but because I know I'll end up yelling "representative!" at a machine that's programmed to ignore me.

The system has made enemies of the people it's supposed to serve and the people it employs to serve them.

The Way Forward

The human cost of our current customer service system is unsustainable. You can't build a service economy on the systematic dehumanization of service workers.

But fixing it requires more than better policies or friendlier scripts. It requires fundamentally changing the economic incentives that created this system.

It requires admitting that customer service is skilled emotional labor that deserves respect, authority, and compensation.

It requires measuring success by human outcomes, not just financial metrics.

It requires treating both customers and workers as full human beings worthy of dignity.

Which brings us to the final piece of our economic puzzle: how all these forces combine to create what I call "the math of misery". The precise calculations that turn human suffering into corporate profit.

Section 5: The Math of Misery

We've seen the profit motive, the budget hierarchy, the technology smokescreen, and the human cost. Now let's look at how all of these forces combine into what I call "the math of misery". The precise calculations that turn customer suffering into corporate profit.

This isn't cruelty. This is mathematics. And the math is brutally elegant.

The Attrition Algorithm

The most profitable insurance companies in the world have figured something out that most people never realize: every claim not paid is profit preserved.

So they've perfected the art of making claims processes just annoying enough, just slow enough, just bureaucratic enough that a predictable percentage of people will give up.

They don't deny claims outright. That would be fraud. Instead, they create friction. They request additional documentation. They require multiple forms. They transfer customers between departments. They put customers on hold for hours.

They're not trying to deny every claim. They're trying to tire out a statistically optimal number of claimants.

Here's the calculation:

- Average claim value: $2,400

- Cost to process claim properly: $180

- Cost to create friction (delays, transfers, requests): $45

- Percentage of customers who give up due to friction: 23%

- Savings per 100 claims: $2,400 × 23 = $55,200

- Additional processing cost: $45 × 100 = $4,500

- Net benefit: $50,700 per 100 claims

The friction pays for itself 11 times over.

The customer service playbook is identical. It's the same math, just applied to post-purchase support instead of insurance claims.

The Deflection Doctrine revisited

Most customer service teams don't measure how well they resolve problems. They measure how well they deflect them.

That word again: "Deflection" is a bureaucrat's synonym for "go away."

I consulted for **MegaRetail** [pseudonym], a Fortune 500 retailer that celebrated achieving a 78% deflection rate. Seventy-eight percent of customers who sought help never spoke to a human being. They measured this as a success metric, not a failure.

"But how many of those customers actually got their problems solved?" I asked.

They produced a self-reported First contact resolution rate of 77%. They have no idea whose problems were actually resolved, just those who never bothered to try again.

They didn't measure that. They measured deflection, not resolution. Because deflection saves money immediately, while resolution quality is harder to track and doesn't impact quarterly budgets.

Here's their math:

- Cost per human interaction: $7.20

- Cost per automated deflection: $0.52

- Annual customer service interactions: 2.4 million

- Deflection rate: 78%

- Deflected interactions: 1,872,000

- Human interactions: 528,000

- Total cost with deflection: ($7.20 × 528,000) + ($0.52 × 1,872,000) = $4,775,040

- Total cost without deflection: $7.20 × 2,400,000 = $17,280,000

- Annual savings: $12,504,960

Twelve and a half million dollars saved by making sure customers can't reach humans.

The fact that frustrated customers might eventually leave the company? That's a future quarter's problem. The cost savings are this quarter's win.

The Escalation Tax

Companies have learned to weaponize their own authority structures.

Want to speak to a supervisor? That's going to cost you time. And time is exactly what companies are betting you don't have.

The average escalation adds 18 minutes to a customer service call. During those 18 minutes, the customer sits on hold while the first-level agent "searches for an available supervisor."

But here's what's really happening: the supervisor isn't busy. The supervisor is waiting the prescribed amount of time to create escalation friction.

I've sat in call centers where supervisors were playing solitaire while customers waited on hold for "supervisor availability." The hold time wasn't operational. It was strategic.

Here's the escalation math:

- Customers who request escalation: 23% of callers
- Customers who abandon during escalation hold: 31%
- Average value of concessions supervisors make: $67
- Escalation abandonment saves: $67 × 31% = $20.77 per escalation request
- Annual escalation requests: 180,000
- Annual savings from escalation abandonment: $3,738,600

Three and three-quarter million dollars saved by making supervisor access artificially scarce.

The Retention Racket

Cancellation departments are profit centers disguised as customer service.

When you try to cancel a subscription, you're not talking to someone whose job is to help you cancel. You're talking to someone whose bonus depends on keeping you subscribed.

Retention specialists are measured on "saves". How many customers they talk out of leaving. Their success metrics have nothing to do with customer satisfaction and everything to do with subscription preservation.

Here's how the retention math works:

- Monthly subscription value: $29.99

- Average customer lifetime if they don't cancel: 18 months

- Value of retained customer: $539.82

- Retention specialist cost per call: $12.50

- Retention success rate: 47%

- Return on Investment per retention attempt: ($539.82 × 47%) - $12.50 = $241.21

That's a 1,931% return on investment for every cancellation call they handle.

So companies make cancellation as difficult as possible:

- Hidden cancellation options on websites

- Phone-only cancellation for services you signed up for online

- Retention offers that restart contract periods

- "Surveys" that are really sales pitches

- Transfer loops between departments

Every additional step in the cancellation process increases the likelihood that customers will give up and remain subscribed.

The Complaint Containment Formula

Companies have sophisticated systems for containing complaints before they become public relations problems.

The complaint containment formula is simple:

- Level 1: Deflect to FAQ or self-service (cost: $0)

- Level 2: Autoresponder acknowledging receipt (cost: $0.03)

- Level 3: Standard response template (cost: $2.40)

- Level 4: Minor concession or credit (cost: $15-50)

- Level 5: Manager call or meaningful resolution (cost: $75-200)

The goal is to resolve as many complaints as possible at Level 1-3, escalating to Level 4-5 only when absolutely necessary to prevent bigger problems.

Here's the containment math:

- Annual complaints: 45,000

- Level 1 resolution: 32% (cost: $0)

- Level 2 resolution: 28% (cost: $378)

- Level 3 resolution: 23% (cost: $2,484)

- Level 4 resolution: 12% (cost: $18,000)

- Level 5 resolution: 5% (cost: $28,125)

- Total complaint handling cost: $48,987

- Cost of handling all complaints at Level 5: $6,750,000

- Savings from containment strategy: $6,701,013

Six point seven million dollars saved by making sure most complaints never get meaningful attention.

The Warranty Workaround

Extended warranties are profit engines built on customer service avoidance.

Companies sell you warranties, then make claiming warranty service so difficult that most people never use them.

I analyzed warranty claim data for a major electronics retailer:

- Extended warranties sold: 340,000 annually

- Average warranty price: $149

- Warranty revenue: $50,660,000

- Warranty claims filed: 12% (40,800)

- Claims actually honored: 67% (27,336)

- Average claim payout: $87

- Total warranty payouts: $2,378,232

- Warranty profit margin: 95.3%

Ninety-five point three percent profit margin because companies collect warranty fees from everyone but only pay claims for a small fraction of customers who successfully navigate the warranty claim process.

The Social Media Cost Avoidance

Social media customer service teams operate under a different math than traditional support channels. But it's still about cost minimization.

Companies respond to social media complaints not because they care more about those customers, but because public complaints have higher potential damage costs.

The social media math:

- Cost per social media response: $3.20

- Cost per phone support interaction: $7.80

- Potential cost of viral negative complaint: $50,000-$500,000

- Social media response rate: 89%

- Phone response rate: 23% (due to deflection)

Social media complaints get attention not because they deserve better service, but because they carry higher financial risk.

The Training Investment Paradox

Companies systematically under-invest in customer service training because agent turnover makes training a negative Return on Investment proposition.

Training investment math:

- Cost to properly train new agent: $2,400

- Average agent tenure: 8.3 months

- Annual training cost per position: $3,470

- Cost of undertrained agent errors: $840 per month

- Annual error cost per position: $10,080

Companies choose the $10,080 in ongoing error costs over the $3,470 in training costs because training is a budget line item this year, while error costs get distributed across multiple departments and quarters.

The Quality Survey Deception

Those satisfaction surveys you get after customer service calls? They're not designed to measure satisfaction. They're designed to generate favorable ratings.

Survey manipulation techniques:

- Ask rating question first, before customers explain their problems

- Use 5-point scales where 4-5 count as "satisfied"

- Survey only customers who had "successful" interactions (avoiding escalations, refunds, complaints)

- Time surveys immediately after resolution, before problems recur

- Weight responses by customer value (VIP opinions count more)

The survey math:

- Actual customer satisfaction: 34%

- Reported customer satisfaction: 78%

- Executive bonuses tied to satisfaction scores: $450,000

- Cost of honest survey methodology: $0

- Value of manipulated results: Priceless (to executives)

The Channel Arbitrage Game

Companies deliberately make some support channels worse than others to force customers into cheaper channels.

Channel cost hierarchy:

- In-person support: $45 per interaction

- Phone support: $7.80 per interaction

- Email support: $3.20 per interaction

- Chat support: $1.90 per interaction

- Self-service: $0.15 per interaction

Channel manipulation strategies:

- Reduce in-person locations and hours

- Increase phone hold times

- Make email response times longer

- Route complex issues to chat (where they can't be resolved)

- Hide phone numbers while promoting self-service

The goal is to push customers down the cost hierarchy, regardless of whether lower-cost channels can actually solve their problems.

The Subscription Trap Algorithm

Subscription businesses have perfected the math of making cancellation harder than signup.

Cancellation friction math:

- Customers who want to cancel: 100%

- Customers who complete easy online cancellation: 94%

- Customers who complete phone-only cancellation: 67%

- Customers who complete complex phone cancellation: 43%

- Customers who complete retention specialist gauntlet: 31%

For every additional step in the cancellation process, companies retain 15-25% more unwilling subscribers.

The Math of Suffering

Add it all up, and you get a system where customer suffering is not just tolerated. It's optimized.

Every minute you wait on hold: calculated

Every transfer between departments: designed

Every request for documentation: strategic

Every "I'm sorry, I can't do that": programmed

The math of misery turns your frustration into their profit margin.

The Breaking Point Economics

But there's one calculation these companies consistently get wrong: the long-term cost of customer rage.

They measure:

- Immediate cost savings from deflection

- Quarterly improvements in efficiency metrics

- Annual reductions in service expenses

They don't measure:

- Lifetime value of customers driven away by poor service

- Word-of-mouth damage from frustrated customers

- Employee turnover costs from demoralized workers

- Regulatory attention attracted by systematic abuse

The math of misery works perfectly, of course until it doesn't.

And increasingly, it doesn't.

Customers are getting angrier. Employees are burning out faster. Regulators are paying attention. Social media amplifies every service failure.

The system that was designed to optimize short-term cost savings is creating long-term value destruction.

The End of the Equation

The math of misery has run its course. The calculations that seemed so elegant, so rational, so financially sound have created a customer service system that serves no one; not customers, not workers, not even the companies that designed it.

Which raises the question: if the current system is mathematically optimized for everyone's suffering, what would a system optimized for everyone's success look like?

That's the question we'll answer in the chapters ahead. Because the same mathematical precision that created this broken system can be used to build something better.

But first, we need to see how these economic forces play out in the real world. Across every industry, in every interaction, with predictable and devastating results.

CHAPTER 4

INDUSTRY SPOTLIGHTS

Section A: Monopolies & Oligopolies

Now that you understand the economic forces driving bad service, let's see how they play out in the real world. Each industry has found its own creative ways to make customer suffering profitable, but the patterns are remarkably consistent based on market structure.

Let's start with the industries where customers have the least choice, and companies have the least incentive to care.

When customers can't leave, companies stop trying to keep them.

Airlines: The Hostage Economy

My connecting flight from Denver to Phoenix was delayed three hours. No explanation. Just "weather."

I looked outside. Clear skies. Not a cloud in sight.

The gate agent, when I could find one, told me to check the app. The app told me to call customer service. Customer service told me to ask the gate agent.

Perfect circle of nobody giving a damn.

Finally, a pilot walking by took pity on me. "Air traffic control backup in Chicago," he said. "Happens every Tuesday. They know about it Monday night but don't tell passengers until you're already at the airport."

That's airlines in a nutshell: They know what's wrong, when it will be fixed, and how it affects you. They just choose not to tell you.

The Economics of Captivity

Airlines discovered something brilliant: once you're past security, you're a hostage. You can't leave. You can't get your money back easily. You can't switch to a competitor because they all suck equally.

So they optimize for everything except your experience.

They'll spend millions on fuel efficiency but won't hire enough gate agents to answer basic questions. They'll invest in new planes but use 1990s computer systems that crash when it rains. They'll give pilots million-dollar training but teach customer service reps to say "I understand you completely" while doing absolutely nothing about it.

The incentive structure is perfectly aligned against you.

When your flight gets canceled, the airline has your money and no obligation to make your day better. They have an obligation to get you to your destination eventually. Maybe tomorrow. Maybe next week. Their computer will find you the next available seat, which might be in a middle seat on a red-eye through three connections.

You'll take it. Because what choice do you have?

The Consolidation Effect

Here's what most people don't realize: the U.S. airline industry isn't really competitive. It's an oligopoly masquerading as a free market.

Four major carriers - American, Delta, Southwest, and United control over 80% of domestic routes. On most city-pair routes, you have two real choices, sometimes one.

This concentration happened gradually through mergers that regulators approved despite obvious anti-competitive effects:

- American merged with US Airways (2013)

- United merged with Continental (2010)

- Delta merged with Northwest (2008)

- Southwest acquired AirTran (2011)

Each merger was justified by promises of "improved efficiency" and "better customer service." Each merger actually reduced competition and degraded service.

When there were more airlines, they had to compete on service because passengers had alternatives. Now they compete on price within an oligopoly structure that makes switching difficult and meaningful choice impossible.

The Frequent Flyer Trap

Airlines have created artificial switching costs through frequent flyer programs that look like customer benefits but actually function as customer prisons.

Once you've accumulated status with one airline, switching means starting over. You lose priority boarding, free checked bags, seat upgrades, lounge access, all the things that make air travel slightly less miserable.

Airlines know this. They deliberately make the base flying experience so awful that their loyalty program benefits feel essential. They've created a protection racket where you pay them (through loyalty) to protect you from the terrible service they provide to non-loyal customers.

A United Premier member gets treated better than a basic economy passenger not because United values loyalty, but because United deliberately treats basic passengers terribly to incentivize program participation.

Why They Get Away With It

Because we let them.

We keep buying tickets based on price, not service. We book the cheapest flight, then act surprised when they treat us like we're worth exactly what we paid.

And honestly? They're not wrong.

If you choose an airline because their ticket is $50 cheaper, you've told them that your dignity is worth $50. They're just taking you at your word.

But here's the deeper problem: even when you're willing to pay more for better service, you often can't find it. When all airlines use the same cost-cutting playbook, paying more just gets you marginally less awful service, not actually good service.

Printer Company

"HP's printer stopped recognizing its own ink cartridges. Their solution? Buy new HP cartridges. When I explained these WERE new HP cartridges, purchased from HP directly, they suggested I was installing them incorrectly. The printer had worked perfectly for three years. Their final suggestion? Buy a new printer."

The Monopoly Advantage

Telecom companies discovered the cheat code to customer service: Be the only option.

In most areas, you have one choice for high-speed internet. Maybe two if you're lucky. So they don't compete on service. Why would they?

They compete on who can be the least terrible while still being profitable. It's a race to the bottom where the bottom keeps moving down.

The infrastructure costs of running cables and cell towers create natural barriers to competition. Once Comcast or Verizon has wired your neighborhood, a competitor would need to invest millions to duplicate that infrastructure for a chance to compete.

Most communities signed exclusive franchise agreements that gave one company monopoly rights in exchange for building infrastructure. These agreements were supposed to be temporary, but they often get renewed automatically.

The result: most Americans have the same choice for high-speed internet that they have for electricity or water. One company, take it or leave it.

The Technical Support Theater

Telecom customer service is performance art. They're not trying to fix your problem, they're performing the ritual of appearing to care about your problem.

The Universal Telecom Script:

- "Have you tried turning it off and on again?"

- "Let me run a diagnostic test." (Types random keys for 2 minutes)

- "I'm seeing some connectivity issues in your area."

- "We can send a technician out next Thursday between 8 AM and 6 PM."

- "There will be a $150 service charge if the problem is with your equipment."

Notice what's missing? Actually looking at your specific issue. Actually trying to solve the problem.

They'd rather send a technician to charge you $150 than spend five minutes checking their network status.

I once worked with a cable company that had real-time network monitoring showing exactly which neighborhoods had outages. But customer service reps weren't given access to this system. They were required to run through the full script even when they could have said, "Yes, there's an outage in your area, we expect it fixed by 3 PM."

Why? Because the script was designed to deflect calls, not resolve problems. If customers knew there was a network outage, they might demand credits for lost service. Better to make them think it might be their equipment.

Why We Stay

Because switching is even worse than staying.

The new company will promise everything. Lower prices, better service, faster speeds. Then you'll spend three weeks without internet while they "install" your service, which means waiting for a technician who may or may not show up in the promised window.

When the technician does show up, they'll tell you the previous company didn't disconnect properly, and you'll need to pay an additional fee to "fix" their work.

So you stay with terrible service because the alternative is potentially worse service plus a month of chaos.

They've weaponized inconvenience.

Utilities: Captive Audience, Captive Service

My power went out during a heat wave. Temperature outside: 107°F.

Called the electric company. After navigating their phone tree, I reached someone who told me to check their website for outage information.

"I can't check the website. My power is out."

"You can use your phone."

"My same phone I used to call you? Yes I checked."

"Is there somewhere else you can go to check the website?"

"I'm calling you to find out about the outage."

Perfect circle of uselessness.

Utilities are regulated monopolies. You can't switch electric companies. You can't shop around for better water service.

So they have zero incentive to provide good customer service. Zero.

You'll pay your bill regardless of how they treat you. You'll use their service regardless of how often it fails. Where else are you going to go?

The regulatory system was supposed to protect consumers by controlling rates and service quality. But regulatory capture means that utilities often have more influence over their regulators than customers do.

State public utility commissions are typically staffed by former utility executives or people hoping to work for utilities in the future. They understand the industry from the utility perspective, not the customer perspective.

Rate hearings are dominated by utility lawyers and consultants who speak the technical language of utility regulation. Customers get three minutes of public comment time to describe how poor service affects their lives.

The Infrastructure Excuse

Utilities love to blame their service problems on "aging infrastructure."

- "We're upgrading our systems." (Translation: Our systems from 1987 don't work well.)

- "We're modernizing our network." (Translation: We should have done this 20 years ago.)

- "We're investing in reliability." (Translation: We've been taking your money without maintaining anything.)

They've had decades to upgrade these systems. They chose not to because... why bother? You can't leave.

The regulated rate structure typically allows utilities to earn a return on capital investments but not on operational improvements. So utilities have incentives to build new infrastructure (which they can charge customers for) but not to maintain existing infrastructure (which comes out of profits).

This creates a perverse incentive to let infrastructure decay until it fails, then seek rate increases to replace it with shiny new infrastructure that generates higher returns.

The Billing Mysteries

Utility bills are incomprehensible by design.

"Energy charge," "delivery charge," "system benefit charge," "renewable energy charge," "customer charge," "demand charge."

Try to get someone to explain what these charges actually mean. They'll read you the definitions from their website, which explain nothing.

"The system benefit charge is a charge for system benefits."

Thanks. That clears it right up.

The complexity isn't accidental. It makes it harder for customers to understand what they're paying for and whether they're being overcharged. It makes it difficult to compare rates between different utilities or different rate structures.

Regulatory compliance requires utilities to publish rate schedules, but they're written in technical language that requires expertise to understand. The average customer has no idea whether they're on the optimal rate schedule for their usage pattern.

Cable/Internet: The Bundling Trap

Cable companies have perfected the art of making it impossible to leave while making it unpleasant to stay.

The bundling trap starts with pricing that makes individual services seem overpriced compared to packages. Want just the internet? That'll be $80/month. Want internet, TV, and phone? That'll be $85/month for the first year.

Of course, the promotional price expires, and your bill doubles in year two. But by then you're locked into a contract with early termination fees that cost more than just staying and paying the higher rate.

The installation process requires taking a day off work to wait for a technician who might show up somewhere in an 8-hour window. The cancellation process requires calling a retention specialist whose job is to make canceling so unpleasant that you give up.

Want to move? You'll need a new installation at your new address, which means another day off work and another round of promotional pricing games.

The equipment rental fees add insult to injury. They'll charge you $15/month to rent a modem that costs $80 to buy. Over a two-year contract, you'll pay $360 to rent a device you could have owned for $80.

But if you buy your own equipment and it doesn't work perfectly, they'll blame every service problem on your "unsupported" device and charge you for service calls.

The Pattern Emerges

Across airlines, telecom, utilities, and cable companies, the pattern is identical:

Market Structure: Limited competition due to infrastructure costs, regulatory barriers, or industry consolidation

Customer Lock-In: High switching costs through contracts, loyalty programs, or monopoly positions

Service Degradation: Once customers are locked in, service quality becomes cost center to be minimized

Complexity as Moat: Billing, policies, and procedures designed to be confusing and discouraging

Regulatory Capture: Industry influence over regulators prevents effective consumer protection

Why Change Doesn't Happen

In truly competitive markets, bad service drives customers to competitors, which eventually forces improvement or bankruptcy.

But in monopolies and oligopolies, market forces don't work. Customers can't vote with their feet because they have nowhere to go.

Political pressure could force change, but most politicians don't experience the customer service systems that torment their constituents. They have staff, corporate accounts, and VIP treatment.

Regulatory pressure could force change, but regulators are often captured by the industries they're supposed to oversee.

The only pressure that works is public embarrassment that threatens brand value or regulatory attention that threatens profit margins.

But these industries have learned to manage negative publicity through crisis communication firms and to manage regulatory threats through lobbying and campaign contributions.

The Captivity Formula

Industries with captive customers follow a predictable pattern:

1. Acquire customers through competitive pricing or exclusive access

2. Lock them in through contracts, switching costs, or eliminating alternatives

3. Degrade service to reduce costs while maintaining lock-in

4. Blame external factors for service failures (weather, regulations, technical complexity)

5. Use pricing games to make leaving seem more expensive than staying

This isn't a conspiracy. It's a rational business strategy in markets where customer choice has been eliminated.

The solution isn't better customer service training or improved technology. It's restoring meaningful customer choice through competition, regulation, or public ownership.

But until that happens, customers in these industries will continue to experience service designed to extract maximum value while providing minimum satisfaction.

When customers can't leave, companies stop trying to keep them happy. They focus on keeping them trapped instead.

And that's exactly what these industries have perfected; the art of profitable captivity disguised as customer service.

Section B: Competitive Markets

You might think that competition would solve the customer service problem. After all, if customers have choices, won't they choose companies that treat them better?

The theory is sound. The reality is more complicated.

In markets with intense price competition, companies face a different set of pressures that can be just as destructive to customer service as monopoly power. When everyone is racing to offer the lowest prices, customer service becomes a luxury that few can afford to provide.

Competition should improve service, but price competition destroys it.

Retail: The Walmart Effect

Walk into any Walmart and you'll see the future of retail customer service: self-checkout kiosks as far as the eye can see, with maybe one human cashier handling the overflow and the customers who can't figure out why the machine keeps saying "unexpected item in bagging area."

This isn't an accident. It's the logical endpoint of competing primarily on price in a low-margin business.

Walmart built the most successful retail empire in history by relentlessly driving down costs and passing the savings to customers. Lower prices meant higher volume. Higher volume meant more leverage with suppliers. More leverage meant even lower costs. The flywheel of efficiency that made everything cheaper for everyone.

Except customer service.

The Labor Equation

Here's the math that drives retail customer service: in a low-margin business, labor is often the largest controllable cost. Food, rent, and utilities are what they are. But retailers can always hire fewer people, pay them less, or make them more "efficient."

Walmart's average profit margin is around 2.4%. That means for every $100 in revenue, they keep $2.40 after all expenses. A single full-time employee making $15/hour costs about $35,000 annually including benefits.

To pay for one additional customer service employee, Walmart needs to generate $1.46 million in additional revenue. That's a lot of customers who need to choose Walmart specifically because of better service rather than lower prices.

But customers don't choose Walmart for service. They choose it for the price. So investing in service employees doesn't generate enough additional revenue to justify the cost.

The result: Walmart optimizes for the customers they have (price-conscious) rather than the customers they could attract (service-conscious) because the math doesn't work for service investment.

Self-checkout isn't customer empowerment. It's labor cost elimination disguised as convenience.

A single employee can now monitor 6-8 self-checkout stations instead of operating one traditional checkout lane. The technology costs are fixed and predictable. The labor savings are immediate and measurable.

But the customer experience? That's transferred from the company to the customer. You now do the work that used to be done for you, and you do it with technology designed for employee efficiency rather than customer experience.

Ever wonder why self-checkout systems are so terrible to use? Because they're not designed for you. They're designed for loss prevention. Every "unexpected item in bagging area" alert and every "please wait for assistance" delay is the system prioritizing inventory control over your convenience.

The few human employees left are spread so thin that getting help means waiting for someone to finish helping three other customers who are also struggling with machines designed to eliminate the need for human help.

Every major retailer has adopted some version of the Walmart playbook because customers vote with their wallets, and most wallets vote for lower prices.

Target tries to differentiate with better design and slightly better service, but they still use self-checkout extensively and staff customer service minimally.

Home Depot puts product expertise into YouTube videos rather than paying for knowledgeable floor staff.

Best Buy eliminated most commission sales positions and replaced them with minimum-wage "product flow" associates who can point you toward products but can't explain why you'd want them.

Amazon took this to its logical extreme: eliminate physical stores entirely and make customers do all the work through websites and apps. When things go wrong, there's no human to talk to in person, just chatbots, email forms, and offshore call centers.

Fast Food: Speed Over Satisfaction

The fast food industry has turned customer service into a precise engineering problem: how to move the maximum number of customers through the system with the minimum labor cost while maintaining acceptable food quality.

Everything is optimized for speed and efficiency rather than customer satisfaction. Drive-through times are measured in seconds. Order accuracy is tracked as a percentage. Customer interactions are scripted to minimize variation and maximize throughput.

The Drive-Through Optimization

Drive-through represents about 70% of fast food sales, and the average target is to serve each customer in under 90 seconds from order to departure.

This time pressure creates a system where customer service becomes customer processing. The goal isn't to make you happy, it's to move you along as quickly as possible so the next customer can be processed.

Got a special request? That slows down the system. Have a question about ingredients? That's not in the script. Want to modify an order after placing it? That requires a manager override that defeats the efficiency metrics.

The drive-through headset operator is often taking orders from multiple customers simultaneously while coordinating with kitchen staff and payment processing. They're not focused on your individual experience, they're managing a complex workflow where you're one variable in an optimization equation.

The Franchise Distance Problem

Most fast food restaurants are franchises, which creates a fundamental disconnect between brand promises and local execution.

McDonald's corporate can create national advertising campaigns about customer satisfaction and "We're lovin' it," but they don't control the day-to-day customer experience. That's controlled by franchise owners who are focused on local profit margins and operational efficiency.

Franchise owners make money by controlling costs and maximizing volume. Customer service training costs money and takes time away from order-taking. Empowering employees to solve problems costs money and creates operational complexity.

So franchise owners implement the minimum customer service required by their franchise agreement and focus on the metrics that directly impact their bottom line: speed, accuracy, and labor costs.

The Technology Replacement Strategy

Fast food chains are rapidly implementing technology to replace human interaction entirely:

- Kiosks for ordering that eliminate cashier positions

- Apps that let customers order ahead and skip human interaction

- Kitchen automation that reduces the need for cooking skills

- AI-powered drive-through systems that take orders without human involvement

The technology is presented as customer convenience, but the real goal is labor cost reduction. A kiosk doesn't call in sick, doesn't need health insurance, doesn't ask for raises, and can work 24/7.

But when the kiosk breaks or doesn't understand your order, there's often no human readily available to help because the staffing model assumes the technology will work perfectly.

E-commerce: Scale vs. Service

Amazon is the ultimate example of how competitive advantage through scale and efficiency can systematically eliminate human customer service.

Amazon's dominance comes from being able to offer the widest selection at competitive prices with fast, reliable delivery. They've achieved this through massive scale, sophisticated logistics, and ruthless operational efficiency.

But human-based customer service? That's a cost center that doesn't contribute to the core competitive advantages of selection, price, and speed.

The Marketplace Responsibility Problem

Most of what you buy on Amazon isn't sold by Amazon. It's sold by third-party merchants using Amazon's platform. This creates a customer service nightmare disguised as convenience.

When something goes wrong with a marketplace purchase, who's responsible? Amazon will tell you to contact the seller. The seller will tell you to go through Amazon. Both have legitimate points about where responsibility lies, but you're stuck in the middle with a problem nobody wants to own.

Amazon has enough market power that they can usually force sellers to provide refunds or replacements when customers complain. But the process often involves multiple contacts, contradictory information, and delays while the two sides sort out who pays for the solution.

The Automation-First Philosophy

Amazon approaches customer service with the same philosophy they apply to warehouses: automate everything possible, use humans only for exceptions.

Their customer service phone number is deliberately hidden on the website. Most issues are routed through help pages, automated systems, and chatbots designed to resolve problems without human involvement.

When you do reach a human, they're often overseas contractors with limited authority and no access to the internal systems that could actually solve complex problems.

Amazon's customer service strategy isn't about making customers happy. It's about efficiently processing customer issues at the lowest possible cost while maintaining just enough satisfaction to prevent customers from switching to competitors.

The Prime Service Tier Strategy

Amazon Prime represents a different approach: explicitly creating service tiers where better service requires additional payment.

Prime members get faster shipping, easier returns, and priority customer service. Non-Prime members get standard shipping, more restrictive return policies, and basic customer service.

This model acknowledges that good service costs money and makes customers pay for it directly rather than building it into product prices. It's more honest than pretending that great service is "included" when it's actually not.

But it also creates a two-tier system where customers who can afford to pay extra get dramatically better treatment than those who can't.

Streaming: The Fragmentation Problem

The streaming industry represents a new take on old customer service problems. These are technology companies that often treat customer service as an afterthought because their primary focus is content acquisition and platform development.

Netflix, Hulu, Disney+, Apple TV+, Amazon Prime Video, HBO Max, Paramount+. Each has its own app, its own billing system, its own customer service approach, and its own technical problems.

The Content Competition Distraction

Streaming companies compete primarily on content, who has the best shows, the most movies, the exclusive series that everyone's talking about.

Customer service doesn't create content differentiation. Nobody chooses Netflix because their customer support is better than Disney's. They choose based on whether Netflix has the shows they want to watch.

This creates a dynamic where customer service budgets compete directly with content acquisition budgets. Every dollar spent on customer service representatives is a dollar not spent on the next big series that might attract new subscribers.

The Technology-First Mentality

Streaming companies are fundamentally technology companies that happen to deliver entertainment. Their executives come from tech backgrounds where customer service is traditionally seen as a cost to be minimized through better product design rather than human support.

The assumption is that if the technology works properly, customers shouldn't need customer service. Problems are seen as temporary bugs to be fixed through engineering rather than ongoing relationships to be managed through human interaction.

When customers do need help, it's often routed through email systems, help centers, and chatbots designed by engineers for other engineers. The support assumes a level of technical literacy that many customers don't have.

The Subscription Trap Problem

Like many modern businesses, streaming services make it easy to subscribe and difficult to cancel. The business model depends on subscription inertia; customers who keep paying for services they're not actively using.

Customer service becomes a retention tool rather than a support function. When customers try to cancel, they're routed to retention specialists whose job is to offer discounts, free months, or plan changes to prevent cancellation.

The goal isn't to help customers make the best decision for their needs. It's to preserve monthly recurring revenue by making cancellation more difficult than just continuing to pay.

The Universal Competitive Pressure

Across retail, fast food, e-commerce, and streaming, the competitive pressure creates similar customer service problems:

Price Competition: When customers choose primarily based on price, investing in service doesn't generate sufficient return on investment

Scale Advantages: Large companies can offer lower prices through economies of scale, but those same efficiencies often eliminate personal service

Technology Substitution: Automation and self-service reduce labor costs but transfer work to customers and eliminate human problem-solving

Operational Focus: Companies optimize for internal efficiency metrics rather than customer experience outcomes

Short-term Thinking: Quarterly financial pressure prioritizes immediate cost reduction over long-term relationship building

The Competitive Paradox

The irony is that in truly competitive markets, exceptional customer service could be a powerful differentiator. But the pressure to compete on price prevents companies from investing in the service differentiation that might allow them to charge higher prices.

This creates a prisoner's dilemma where every company would benefit if all companies invested in better service and competed on value rather than price. But any individual company that invests in service while competitors cut costs will be at a short-term disadvantage.

The Customer Complicity

Customers enable this race to the bottom by consistently choosing lower prices over better service when given the choice.

We shop at Walmart despite knowing the customer service is minimal because the prices are lower.

We order from Amazon despite knowing we'll have to navigate automated systems for support because the convenience and selection are better.

We eat at fast food restaurants despite knowing the service is scripted and impersonal because it's fast and cheap.

Our revealed preferences tell companies that we value price and convenience more than human customer service. So that's what they optimize for.

The Breaking Point

The competitive market approach to customer service works until it doesn't. Companies can cut service costs and maintain market share as long as competitors are doing the same thing.

But when customer frustration reaches a breaking point, it creates opportunities for companies willing to compete on service rather than just price.

Costco built a successful business model around membership fees that fund better employee treatment, which creates better customer service, which justifies the membership fees.

Zappos (before being acquired by Amazon) built a business around exceptional customer service in online shoe sales, proving that some customers will pay slightly more for significantly better treatment.

In-N-Out Burger competes successfully against McDonald's and other fast food chains by paying employees more, training them better, and creating a customer experience that feels more personal despite being systematic.

The Service Opportunity

In hyper-competitive markets, exceptional customer service can be a sustainable competitive advantage precisely because it's difficult to copy quickly.

Technology can be replicated. Prices can be matched. Distribution can be duplicated.

But service culture, employee training, and customer relationship management take time to build and are harder for competitors to reverse-engineer.

The companies that will succeed in competitive markets are those that find ways to use service as a differentiator rather than treating it as a cost to be minimized.

But this requires customers who are willing to pay for better service and businesses with long-term thinking that can invest in service advantages even when the return isn't immediate.

The Path Forward

Competitive markets don't automatically produce good customer service. They produce the customer service that customers are willing to pay for.

If customers consistently choose lower prices over better service, companies will consistently provide lower prices with worse service.

But if enough customers demand better service and are willing to pay for it, competitive markets can be powerful forces for service innovation and improvement.

The question is whether customers and businesses can break out of the race to the bottom and compete on value creation rather than cost reduction.

Competition should improve service, but only if we compete on the right things.

Section C: Essential Services

If monopolies are bad for customer service and competitive markets are bad for customer service, what about essential services - industries where customers can't really choose not to participate?

Banking, healthcare, insurance, government, these aren't optional for most people. You need a bank account to function in modern society. You need health insurance to avoid financial ruin. You need car insurance to drive legally. You need government services to exist as a citizen.

When customers can't avoid your service, you can avoid serving them.

This creates the most perverse incentives of all: essential service providers can systematically abuse customers because customers have no meaningful alternative to going without the service entirely.

Healthcare: Suffering in Triplicate

My son needed an MRI. Simple enough, right?

First, we called our insurance to confirm it was covered. "Yes, 100% covered after deductible."

Then we called the imaging center. "We'll need prior authorization."

So we called the doctor to request prior authorization. "We'll submit that today. Should be approved by Friday."

Friday comes. No approval. We called the doctor. "Insurance is requesting more documentation."

We call insurance. "We need to see if this is medically necessary."

We called the doctor. "We'll submit additional notes."

Two weeks later, the approval comes through. We schedule the MRI.

The day of the MRI, they tell us our deductible has changed. The procedure will cost $2,400 out of pocket.

We'd already taken time off work, arranged childcare, and fasted for 12 hours. So we did it.

Three weeks later, we got a bill for an additional $800. "Radiologist reading fee not covered."

Nobody mentioned a radiologist reading fee. Apparently, having someone actually look at the MRI results costs extra.

The Deliberate Maze

Healthcare customer service isn't just bad. It's maliciously complicated.

Every step is designed to make you give up. The phone trees, the prior authorizations, the referrals, the co-pays, the deductibles, the "out of network" fees that nobody explains until after the service.

It's not an accident. It's a business model.

The more friction they create, the more people give up before getting care. Every person who gives up is a claim they don't have to pay. Every procedure that gets delayed is money they can invest and earn returns on before paying out.

Insurance companies employ more people to deny claims than to approve them. They have entire departments dedicated to finding reasons why treatments aren't "medically necessary" or why providers are "out of network" or why procedures need additional documentation.

The Information Asymmetry

Healthcare customer service is uniquely awful because customers operate from a position of profound ignorance about what they're buying and what it should cost.

You can research car prices, compare hotel amenities, and read reviews of restaurants. But healthcare pricing is deliberately opaque, quality metrics are impossible to assess, and urgency often prevents shopping around.

Need emergency surgery? You're not going to comparison shop between hospitals while you're bleeding. Your insurance company knows this, the hospital knows this, and they price accordingly.

Even for non-emergency care, try calling different providers to ask what a procedure will cost. You'll get answers like "that depends on your insurance" or "we'll submit the claim and see what they approve" or "you'll need to call the billing department."

The billing department will tell you to call your insurance. Your insurance will tell you to ask the provider for procedure codes. The provider will tell you that coding depends on what the doctor finds during the appointment you haven't had yet.

It's a shell game designed to prevent you from making informed decisions about your own healthcare.

The Empathy Deficit

I once watched a woman at a hospital billing office try to set up a payment plan for her husband's cancer treatment.

The billing rep handed her a form. "Fill this out. We'll need three months of bank statements, two years of tax returns, and a letter from your employer confirming your income."

"How long will this take to process?"

"Six to eight weeks."

"My husband starts chemo next Monday."

The woman started crying. The billing rep started typing.

Not typing anything useful. Just... typing. The universal customer service response to human emotion: ignore it and focus on the screen.

Healthcare customer service is uniquely awful because people's lives depend on it, but the system treats patients like accounting problems to be managed rather than human beings to be healed.

Why It's Unconscionable

Healthcare customer service fails people when they're most vulnerable. When they're sick, scared, or dealing with medical emergencies that affect their families.

Unlike other industries where bad customer service is merely frustrating, healthcare customer service failures can be life-threatening. People die because they can't navigate insurance approvals fast enough. People go bankrupt because they can't understand billing procedures. People suffer because they can't access the care they've already paid for through insurance premiums.

The industry knows this. Everyone in the system knows this. But the incentive is still to create friction, delay care, and make it as hard as possible to access the services people have already paid for.

Banking: Your Money, Their Rules

I tried to deposit a check a few years back. Not cash it, deposit it into my own account.

The teller looked at the check like I'd handed her a dead fish. "This is made out to your business name, but your account is personal."

"It's a sole proprietorship," I explained. "Same taxpayer ID number. Same person."

"I'll need a business license."

"For sole proprietorship? There is no business license."

"Then I'll need a DBA filing."

"I don't have a DBA. It's not required for this"

"I'm sorry, I can't help you without proper documentation."

Twenty minutes later, the manager overrode it with one keystroke. One keystroke that the teller was forbidden to use because... reasons.

The Technology Theater

Banks love to brag about their apps. "Bank from anywhere! Deposit checks with your phone!"

Then you try to do anything meaningful and the app says, "For your security, please visit a branch or call customer service."

So you call customer service. They say, "For your security, we'll need to transfer you to our verification department."

The verification department says, "For your security, we recommend you visit a branch with two forms of ID."

At the branch, they look at your ID and say, "This should be easy to do in the app."

The circle of bureaucratic hell.

Why It's Particularly Offensive

Banks are special because they're holding your money while treating you like a criminal for wanting to access it.

They're not providing a service. They're gatekeeping your own cash and charging you for the privilege.

And when things go wrong, when they overdraft you by mistake, when their system double-charges you, when their security freeze locks you out of your own account. They act like they're the victims.

"We're just following procedures." "It's for your protection." "Our systems are down."

No, their systems are fine. Their priorities are broken.

Banks profit from the float. The time between when you deposit money and when you can access it, between when they withdraw payment and when it leaves their account. They earn interest on your money while making you wait to use it.

The bureaucracy isn't incompetence. It's profitable incompetence designed to maximize the time your money stays in their control.

Insurance: The Professional "No" Industry

I had a minor fender-bender. The other driver was clearly at fault; ran a red light, hit my car, admitted fault to the police.

Called my insurance company to report it. They were helpful, understanding, and efficient.

Called the other driver's insurance company to file a claim. Different experience entirely.

"We'll need to investigate to determine fault."

"The police report says your driver ran a red light."

"We'll need to review all available evidence."

"There's video from the traffic camera."

"We'll need to have our adjuster examine both vehicles."

"Your driver admitted fault."

"We'll be in touch once our investigation is complete."

Six weeks later: "We've determined our driver was 50% at fault. We'll pay 50% of your damages."

"How is running a red light 50% fault?"

"You could have avoided the accident by driving more defensively."

"I had a green light."

"We're only authorized to offer 50%."

The Adversarial Model

Insurance companies have perfected the art of taking your money while fighting every claim.

They'll spend more money on lawyers to deny your claim than it would cost to just pay it. Not because it makes financial sense for your individual claim, but because it sends a message to other customers: We will fight you on everything.

Every claim becomes a negotiation where the insurance company starts from a position that they owe you nothing and forces you to prove otherwise. Even when you have documentation, witnesses, and obvious evidence of what happened.

The Delay Tactics

Insurance customer service is designed around delay.

They'll request the same documents multiple times. They'll ask for additional information just as you think you're done. They'll schedule inspections, then reschedule them. They'll transfer your case to different adjusters who need to "review everything from the beginning."

Every delay is intentional. They're hoping you'll get frustrated and accept a lower settlement. Or better yet, give up entirely.

The money they're not paying you is money they can invest and earn returns on. Every month they delay payment is another month of investment income. The interest they earn on delayed claims often exceeds the administrative cost of creating the delays.

The Magic Words

Insurance companies have trained their customer service reps to use specific phrases that sound helpful but mean nothing:

- "We're investigating your claim." (Translation: We're stalling.)

- "We need additional documentation." (Translation: We're stalling.)

- "Your claim is being reviewed by our specialists." (Translation: We're stalling.)

- "We want to make sure you get a fair settlement." (Translation: We're stalling.)

The words change, but the strategy is the same: delay, deflect, deny.

Government: The Taliban Has Customer Service

The Taliban posted a customer service number.

You read that right.

In the same week they retook control of Afghanistan, they published a hotline for complaints. It was basic. A number. A promise. "We will listen."

Now, I can't speak to the actual quality of that experience. I didn't get past the language barrier. But I can tell you this: I've waited longer on hold with my local Department of Motor Vehicles than it took for that call to go through.

Let that sink in.

We live in a country where your DMV has less urgency than a regime with 14th-century values. They may not believe in women's rights, but they do believe in contact centers.

Why? Because even they understand that service is power. Access is influence. A working phone number is a show of control.

The Designed Friction

Our agencies aren't broken by accident. They're built to be slow. Built to be confusing. Built to bleed your time, not just your patience. Friction isn't a side effect, it's a feature.

You're not in line. You're in a filter. The system isn't trying to serve everyone. It's trying to shake some of you off.

I was in a beige conference room in Tallahassee, surrounded by agency lifers in stiff suits and stiff expressions. We were presenting data on the average wait time to initiate unemployment benefits: two hours and eighteen minutes. One guy leaned back in his chair, hands behind his head, and said:

"If my kids were hungry, I'd wait four hours."

And that was the moment I knew we weren't fixing anything. Not today. Maybe not ever.

See, in the private sector, they make you wait because service costs money. In the public sector? They make you wait because urgency threatens the machinery. The system isn't just slow, it's built slow. It's designed to discourage, dissuade, deter. A little pain to weed out the "unserious."

The Complexity Advantage

We once audited the call logs of a state agency responsible for food benefits. They had a four-digit menu tree, which meant a caller could press up to 10 buttons before speaking to a human. If they pressed the wrong combo? The system would hang up. No warning. Just darkness.

And when we brought this up? A deputy director said, "That's working as designed. We get fewer nuisance calls."

What they call a nuisance is what most people call survival.

Government customer service complexity isn't bureaucratic incompetence. It's bureaucratic competence designed to reduce demand for services by making access to those services prohibitively difficult.

Government Employees Are Hostages Too

Let's talk about Alec. He's the DMV rep you met at 7:42 a.m., just after you grabbed Number 34. You watched Alec handle your husband's case. Then you tried to walk up, only to be told you'd need to wait again. Another hour. He "put your name back in the system."

You were furious. And I get it.

But Alec didn't wake up that morning hoping to ruin your day. He works in a broken building, under a broken process, with broken systems, and gets yelled at by broken people every 15 minutes.

The truth? Alec gave up months ago.

We interviewed dozens of people like him, public servants, many of whom joined their agencies with a fire to do good. That fire lasted, on average, 120 days. After that? Smoldering apathy.

Like Mia, a child welfare caseworker who showed up to our focus group in a hoodie that said "Unbothered." She'd been on the job 11 months and already knew: "No one above me listens, and the system below me breaks people. So I work my wage."

She wasn't lazy. She was resigned.

The system fails its own employees before it ever fails you. It gives them outdated tech, unclear authority, and performance metrics that punish them for showing initiative. Over time, they stop trying. They start using the same phrases the IVRs do.

"We can't do that here." "You'll need to call the state office." "You should try the website."

They're not being cruel. They're being trained.

The Power Imbalance

What makes essential services uniquely awful is the fundamental power imbalance between provider and customer.

In other industries, customer dissatisfaction eventually creates business consequences. Lost revenue, competitive disadvantage, market share decline.

But essential service providers face no meaningful market consequences for customer dissatisfaction because customers can't meaningfully exit the market.

Healthcare: You can't choose not to get sick. Insurance is tied to employment for most people. Provider networks limit choice even when you have options.

Banking: You need bank accounts for employment, housing, basic commerce. Switching banks is complex and time-consuming. Credit relationships take years to build.

Insurance: Often required by law (auto insurance) or practical necessity (health insurance). Claims history affects future insurability.

Government: You can't choose not to be a citizen. Government services are often monopolies by design. Political processes for change are slow and uncertain.

The Regulatory Capture Problem

Essential services are often heavily regulated, which should protect customers but often protects providers instead.

Regulatory agencies are typically staffed by people from the industries they regulate or people hoping to work in those industries. They speak the technical language of the industry, understand its constraints and challenges, and often view their role as helping the industry manage regulatory compliance rather than protecting customers from industry abuse.

Customer voices in regulatory processes are often drowned out by industry lobbying, technical complexity, and procedural barriers that favor sophisticated participants over individual consumers.

Banking regulators focus on systemic financial stability rather than individual customer experience. Insurance regulators focus on company solvency rather than claims processing fairness. Healthcare regulators focus on clinical outcomes rather than administrative burden.

The Compliance Theater

Essential service providers have learned to use regulatory compliance as customer service theater.

"We're required by federal regulations to..." becomes the excuse for any policy that customers find objectionable, regardless of whether the regulation actually requires the specific implementation the company chose.

"For your protection..." becomes the justification for any procedure that protects the company more than the customer.

"This is industry standard..." becomes the defense against any criticism, as if industry-wide bad practices justify individual company bad practices.

The regulatory framework creates a shield that essential service providers use to deflect responsibility for customer service failures while maintaining the appearance of being constrained by external forces beyond their control.

The Systemic Nature

Essential services create customer service problems that go beyond individual company policies or market dynamics.

When entire industries can systematically abuse customers without facing market consequences, it creates broader social and economic problems:

Trust erosion: People lose faith in institutions that are supposed to serve them but consistently prioritize their own interests instead.

Economic inefficiency: Time and resources spent fighting with essential service providers is time and resources not spent on productive activities.

Social inequality: People with more resources, education, and connections can navigate complex systems more easily, while vulnerable populations face higher barriers to accessing services they need.

Political dysfunction: When government services don't work, people lose faith in the government's ability to solve problems, creating political pressure for privatization that often makes problems worse rather than better.

The Way Forward

Essential services could provide excellent customer service if the incentives were aligned properly. Some examples exist:

Credit unions often provide better banking customer service than traditional banks because they're owned by their members rather than shareholders.

Medicare often provides more straightforward healthcare administration than private insurance because it doesn't profit from denying claims.

Some utilities in areas with effective public oversight provide reliable service with reasonable customer support because regulatory pressure creates accountability.

But these examples are exceptions that prove the rule: essential service providers will provide good customer service only when they face meaningful consequences for providing bad service.

The Accountability Gap

The fundamental problem with essential services is the accountability gap between the people who make policy decisions and the people who experience the consequences of those decisions.

Healthcare executives have concierge medical care and don't experience the insurance maze they create for other people.

Banking executives have private banking relationships and don't experience the fee structures and bureaucracy they impose on other customers.

Government officials have staff who handle their personal interactions with government agencies and don't experience the systems they oversee.

Insurance executives have legal departments that handle their personal claims and don't experience the delay tactics they deploy against other customers.

Without personal accountability to the systems they create, essential service providers have no incentive to make those systems work for the people who depend on them.

The Human Cost Multiplier

Bad customer service in essential services creates cascading human costs that go far beyond inconvenience.

People die because they can't navigate healthcare bureaucracy fast enough to get life-saving treatment.

People lose homes because they can't resolve banking errors before mortgage payments are due.

People face legal problems because they can't access government services required for compliance with other regulations.

People lose their livelihoods because they can't get insurance claims processed in time to repair business equipment or property.

The stakes are higher in essential services, but the quality is often lower precisely because the high stakes reduce customer alternatives rather than increasing provider accountability.

The Power to Change

Essential services can be fixed, but only through changes that restore accountability and consequences for poor performance.

Market-based solutions work only when customers have real alternatives and real choice.

Regulatory solutions work only when regulators prioritize customer outcomes over industry preferences.

Political solutions work only when politicians face consequences for the customer service failures of the agencies and industries they oversee.

The power to change essential services lies with customers who organize collectively to demand better treatment and politicians who face electoral consequences for allowing systematic abuse to continue.

Individual customer complaints disappear into a bureaucratic void. But organized customer pressure, media attention, and political consequences can force change even in industries that seem immune to customer feedback.

Essential services prove that when customers can't avoid you, you can avoid serving them, unless customers organize to make avoidance impossible and accountability unavoidable.

When you can't live without them, they have no reason to live up to their promises. Unless we give them one.

Conclusion: The Universal Truths

After touring this wasteland of customer service failure across monopolies, competitive markets, and essential services, several patterns emerge that transcend industry boundaries.

These aren't accidents. These aren't oversights. These are deliberate business decisions that prioritize short-term cost savings over long-term customer relationships, enabled by market structures that eliminate meaningful customer choice or accountability.

Let me state the universal truths plainly:

Truth #1: When customers have no choice, service disappears

Monopolies, oligopolies, and essential services provide the worst customer service because they can. Whether it's airlines trapping you past security, telecom companies enjoying infrastructure monopolies, or government agencies controlling access to essential services, the pattern is identical: eliminate customer alternatives, then systematically reduce service quality to maximize extraction while minimizing cost.

The math is brutal but rational. Why invest in customer satisfaction when customers can't leave? Why solve problems quickly when delays don't create competitive disadvantage? Why empower frontline workers when customer complaints have no business consequences?

Truth #2: When service is "included" in the price, it gets minimized

Every company tells you that customer service is "included" as if it's a free bonus. But nothing is free. Service costs are baked into pricing, which means they become costs to be minimized rather than value to be maximized.

This creates the fundamental misalignment that drives every customer service failure: companies want to provide the minimum service necessary to prevent customer exodus while customers paid for the service level they expected when they made the purchase.

In competitive markets, this race to the bottom becomes systematic as companies compete on price while cutting service costs. In non-competitive markets, companies can simply pocket the service savings without fear of customer departure.

Truth #3: When technology avoids customers instead of serving them, everyone loses

Every industry we examined uses technology the same way: to deflect customer contact rather than improve customer outcomes. Phone trees designed to exhaust you, chatbots programmed to minimize escalation, apps that transfer work from companies to customers.

The technology exists to provide incredible customer service - instant access to information, personalized solutions, predictive problem-solving. But it's deployed to avoid providing service rather than enhance it because avoiding customers is cheaper than serving them.

This creates the perverse outcome where technological advancement makes customer service worse instead of better. We have more sophisticated tools for customer avoidance than any previous generation, disguised as customer empowerment and digital transformation.

Truth #4: When frontline workers have no authority to solve problems, they become professional apologizers

Across every industry, frontline customer service workers are systematically disempowered to actually help customers. They can apologize, empathize, and transfer, but they can't solve, decide, or act.

This isn't incompetence, it's design. Companies deliberately remove authority from the people customers talk to in order to control costs, prevent "unauthorized" solutions, and maintain policy compliance.

The result is customer service theater where workers perform helpfulness while being structurally prevented from providing help. Customers get frustrated with individual workers who are themselves victims of systems designed to prevent effective customer service.

Truth #5: When companies view customer service as a cost center instead of a competitive advantage, it becomes a competitive disadvantage

The most revealing pattern across all industries is how customer service is budgeted, measured, and managed as a cost to be minimized rather than an investment to be optimized.

Marketing gets measured on customer acquisition. Sales gets measured on revenue generation. Product development gets measured on feature delivery. Customer service gets measured on cost per interaction, average handle time, and deflection rates.

When you measure customer service by how little it costs rather than how much value it creates, you get customer service designed to cost as little as possible regardless of the value it destroys.

This creates a vicious cycle where bad service increases the cost of service (more angry customers, more complex problems, more escalations) while reducing the value of service (lower satisfaction, higher churn, negative word-of-mouth).

The Meta-Truth: The System Is Working as Designed

The most important pattern is that none of these failures are accidental. They're the predictable result of economic incentives that reward customer avoidance and punish customer satisfaction.

Every industry has discovered that they can increase short-term profitability by systematically degrading customer service until they reach the point where further degradation would cost more in lost customers than it saves in operational efficiency.

This optimization point varies by industry based on customer alternatives, switching costs, and competitive dynamics. But every industry finds their optimal level of customer dissatisfaction and systematically maintains it.

Airlines optimize for the maximum level of customer misery that doesn't trigger passenger revolts or regulatory intervention.

Telecom companies optimize for the maximum level of service failure that doesn't cause customers to endure the pain of switching providers.

Banks optimize for the maximum level of bureaucratic friction that doesn't cause customers to go through the complexity of changing their financial relationships.

Healthcare companies optimize for the maximum level of administrative burden that doesn't cause patients to forgo necessary care or employers to change insurance providers.

This isn't broken. This is advanced optimization for the wrong objectives.

The Competitive Disadvantage Paradox

Here's the irony: in an economy where products are increasingly commoditized and differentiation is difficult, customer service should be the ultimate competitive advantage.

When cars perform similarly, hotels offer similar amenities, and banks provide similar financial products, the quality of customer service should be the deciding factor for customer choice.

But companies have collectively decided to compete on everything except customer service. They compete on price, features, marketing, distribution, technology. Everything except the one thing that could create sustainable competitive advantage and genuine customer loyalty.

This creates enormous opportunities for companies willing to break ranks and compete on customer experience. The bar is so low that providing merely competent service feels revolutionary to customers who have been systematically trained to expect incompetence.

The Trust Erosion

The universal degradation of customer service is creating broader social and economic costs that don't show up in quarterly financial reports but show up in social cohesion, institutional trust, and economic productivity.

When every interaction with large institutions involves fighting through systems designed to frustrate you, people lose faith in the institutions themselves. When companies systematically break promises they make to customers, people lose faith in market-based solutions to social problems. When technology is consistently used to make human interactions worse rather than better, people lose faith in technological progress.

Customer service is the front line of the relationship between institutions and individuals. When that relationship becomes systematically adversarial, it affects everything else, trust in government, faith in markets, belief in corporate responsibility, confidence in technological solutions.

The Hidden Costs

The customer service crisis creates enormous hidden costs that companies externalize to customers and society:

Economic costs: Millions of hours of human productivity lost to fighting with customer service systems that don't work

Social costs: Erosion of trust between institutions and the people they're supposed to serve

Innovation costs: Resources spent on customer avoidance technology instead of customer service technology

Human costs: Stress, frustration, and demoralization for both customers and frontline workers

Opportunity costs: Companies that could differentiate through service but choose to compete on cost reduction instead

These costs don't appear on any company's income statement, but they appear in reduced economic productivity, increased social inequality, and decreased institutional legitimacy.

The Breaking Point

Customer service can't get infinitely worse without consequences. Every system has breaking points where further optimization in the wrong direction creates catastrophic failure rather than incremental improvement.

We're approaching several breaking points simultaneously:

Customer tolerance: People are increasingly unwilling to accept terrible service as the price of modern commerce

Worker tolerance: Frontline service workers are quitting in record numbers rather than absorb customer rage while being powerless to help

Technology limits: Automation is reaching the limits of what it can do without human judgment and empathy

Regulatory attention: Politicians are beginning to pay attention to customer service failures as constituents demand action

Competitive pressure: In some industries, companies are discovering they can gain significant market advantage by providing merely competent service while competitors provide terrible service

The Path Forward

The universal truths reveal both the problem and the solution.

The problem is systematic misalignment of incentives that reward customer avoidance while punishing customer satisfaction across all market structures.

The solution is systematic realignment of incentives that make customer satisfaction profitable while making customer avoidance expensive.

This requires changes in:

- How we measure service success (customer outcomes rather than company costs)

- How we deploy technology (to enhance human capability rather than replace human contact)

- How we structure markets (to preserve meaningful customer choice and competition)

- How we regulate essential services (to prioritize customer outcomes over industry convenience)

- How we allocate corporate resources (to treat service as investment rather than expense)

But most importantly, it requires recognizing that customer service failures aren't inevitable consequences of modern scale and complexity. They're deliberate choices made by rational actors optimizing for rational objectives within systems that reward the wrong things.

Change those systems, and you change the outcomes.

The Question That Remains

If the patterns are so clear and the solutions are so obvious, why does the system persist? Why don't market forces correct customer service failures? Why don't companies invest in the competitive advantages that customer service could provide?

Why, in other words, does nothing change despite universal dissatisfaction with the current system?

The answer requires understanding not just why bad customer service exists, but why it persists despite making everyone, customers, workers, and ultimately companies themselves worse off.

That's where our journey takes us next: into the forces that maintain broken systems even when everyone involved knows they're broken and could be fixed.

Because understanding why nothing changes is the key to making everything change.

CHAPTER 5

WHY NOTHING CHANGES

Section 1: Customer Complicity

Everyone hates the current system. Customers are miserable. Workers are burned out. Even executives privately admit customer service is terrible. The technology exists to fix it. The economic case for change is clear.

So why does nothing change?

Let's start with an uncomfortable truth: We're not just victims of bad customer service. We're accomplices.

Let me tell the truth for once. We like to act shocked. Outraged. Indignant. But we're not innocent. We keep rewarding the worst behavior in customer service like it's a damn game show. And then we wonder why nothing changes.

The Spirit Airlines Paradox

Who's the worst airline in America?

If you didn't just think "Spirit," you haven't been paying attention. Spirit Airlines has turned terrible customer service into an art form. They charge you to pick your seat. They charge you to bring a carry-on bag. They charge you to print your boarding pass at the airport. They pack seats so tightly that your knees touch your chin. Their planes are flying buses with wings.

In December 2023, Spirit Airlines lost a kid. A literal child. An unaccompanied minor was sent to the wrong city. And you'd think, "Surely this is it. This is where people draw the line."

Nope.

Customers kept booking.

If people have to swipe a credit card to use the bathroom they will still go back. Folks who've had to pay to print a boarding pass keep returning. Passengers who've been stranded overnight with no assistance continue choosing Spirit for their next trip.

Why? Because Spirit flights cost $89 instead of $189.

That's not broken customer logic. That's math. Customers have calculated that saving $100 is worth being treated like livestock. Spirit knows this, so they optimize for exactly that trade-off.

But here's where it gets interesting: these same customers who voluntarily choose cattle-car treatment then rage on social media about being treated like cattle. They write scathing reviews about services they consciously purchased. They complain bitterly about experiences they paid money to have.

You can't buy the cheapest possible airline ticket and then act surprised when you get the cheapest possible experience.

The Revealed Preference Problem

Economists have a concept called "revealed preference", the idea that what people actually do tells you more about their true preferences than what they say they want.

We say we want great customer service. But our revealed preferences tell a different story.

We shop at Walmart despite knowing the customer service is minimal because the prices are lower.

We bank with institutions that treat us like account numbers because they don't charge monthly fees.

We get our phones from companies that make us wait on hold for hours because their plans are $20 cheaper.

We eat at restaurants that treat us like order numbers because the food comes faster and costs less.

Our purchasing decisions send a clear signal to companies: we value price and convenience more than human customer service. So that's what they optimize for.

The Price vs. Service Choice

Every day, customers face choices between companies that compete on price and companies that compete on service. Almost every time, we choose price.

Retail: Target offers slightly better customer service than Walmart, but Walmart's prices are lower. Where do most people shop? Walmart has 2.3 million employees. Target has 400,000.

Banking: Credit unions typically offer better customer service than major banks. More personal attention, fewer fees, humans who know your name. But big banks offer more ATMs, better apps, and more convenient locations. Where do most people bank? Bank of America has 66 million customers. The largest credit union has 6 million.

Telecommunications: Local internet providers often offer better customer service than Comcast or Verizon. Local support, faster problem resolution, people you can actually talk to. But the big companies offer faster speeds, broader coverage, and bundled pricing. Who has more customers?

Food: Local restaurants typically offer better service than chain restaurants. Servers who remember your preferences, owners who care about your experience, flexibility with special requests. But chains offer predictable quality, faster service, and lower prices. Which business model dominates the industry?

The pattern is clear: when customers have to choose between price and service, they choose price. Companies learned this lesson and optimized accordingly.

The Switching Cost Excuse

When confronted with this pattern, customers often blame "switching costs". The hassle and expense of changing providers.

"I'd love to leave Comcast, but switching is such a pain."

"I know my bank treats me terribly, but moving all my accounts would take forever."

"I hate my phone company, but I don't want to deal with transferring my number and learning a new system."

These switching costs are real. But let's be honest about the math.

If you spend 4 hours a year fighting with your current service provider, and switching would take 8 hours upfront, you break even in 2 years. Most customer relationships last much longer than 2 years.

If terrible service costs you $50 a year in wasted time and frustration, and switching costs you $100 upfront, you break even in 2 years and save money every year after that.

The switching cost excuse often doesn't hold up to analysis. The real reason people don't switch is that the alternatives aren't actually much better. When all companies in an industry use the same cost-cutting playbook, switching doesn't solve the problem. It just trades one set of frustrations for another.

The Walmart Effect on Everything

Walmart didn't become the world's largest retailer by accident. They built the most successful business model in history by obsessively focusing on one thing: offering the lowest prices possible.

Lower prices required lower costs. Lower costs meant more efficient operations, better supplier negotiations, and yes, minimal customer service.

Walmart's success taught every other industry that customers will accept worse service in exchange for lower prices. This lesson has been applied everywhere:

Airlines: Southwest built a hugely successful business by stripping out all the service elements that cost money. Assigned seats, meal service, premium amenities; and passing the savings to customers through lower fares.

Hotels: Budget hotel chains eliminated room service, concierge assistance, and other high-touch services to offer rooms at half the price of full-service hotels.

Banking: Online banks eliminated branch networks and human customer service to offer higher interest rates and lower fees.

Retail: Discount retailers eliminated sales assistance, store ambiance, and return flexibility to offer lower prices on identical products.

Each industry discovered the same thing Walmart discovered: a large segment of customers will accept significantly worse service for modestly lower prices.

The Amazon Acceleration

Amazon took the Walmart model and supercharged it with technology and scale.

Amazon's customer service is designed around one principle: make it as cheap as possible while maintaining just enough customer satisfaction to prevent customers from switching to competitors.

Most customer service interactions are routed through automated systems, help pages, and chatbots. When you do reach a human, they're often overseas contractors with limited authority and no access to the internal systems that could actually solve complex problems.

But customers accept this because Amazon offers unmatched selection, competitive pricing, and incredibly fast delivery. The customer service tradeoff feels worth it for the other benefits.

Amazon's success has taught every other company that customers will tolerate that brand of customer service if other parts of the value proposition are strong enough.

The Subscription Model Complicity

The subscription economy has created a new form of customer complicity: paying for services we don't use because canceling is more hassle than the monthly fee.

Gym memberships, streaming services, software subscriptions, meal kit deliveries companies have learned that they can make more money from customer inertia than customer satisfaction.

The business model depends on customers who sign up enthusiastically and then gradually stop using the service but don't bother to cancel it. Customer service becomes a retention tool rather than a support function designed to make canceling more difficult than continuing to pay.

Customers enable this model by accepting the cancellation friction as normal rather than demanding easier exit options. We've normalized the idea that signing up should be easy while canceling should be hard.

The Gratitude Trap

Perhaps the most insidious form of customer complicity is how we've learned to be grateful for basic competence.

When a company provides merely adequate customer service, we're so surprised that we leave glowing reviews and tell all our friends about the "amazing" experience.

A hotel that has clean rooms and working WiFi gets praised for excellent service. A restaurant where the server is polite and the food arrives warm gets celebrated on social media. A customer service rep who solves your problem in one call becomes a hero worthy of a LinkedIn post.

This isn't because these experiences are objectively excellent. It's because our expectations have been systematically lowered by so many terrible experiences that basic competence feels miraculous.

Companies have learned that they don't need to provide genuinely great service, they just need to be slightly less terrible than their competitors to earn customer loyalty and positive word-of-mouth.

The Network Effect Problem

Customer complicity becomes self-reinforcing through network effects. The more people use inferior services, the more valuable those services become despite their quality problems.

Everyone uses Facebook despite knowing their customer service is terrible because that's where all their friends and family are.

Everyone shops on Amazon despite the customer service limitations because that's where all the products, ease of return and reviews are.

Everyone flies the major airlines despite their service problems because they have the most routes and frequent flyer programs.

These network effects make it rational for individual customers to choose services they know are inferior because the network value outweighs the service quality problems.

The Busy Life Defense

Modern customers often defend their complicity by pointing to time constraints and busy lifestyles.

"I don't have time to research alternatives to Amazon. I just need to order something and get it delivered quickly."

"I don't have the bandwidth to deal with switching banks. My current bank is terrible, but at least I know how terrible it is."

"I can't spend my weekend comparing customer service policies. I just want to buy what I need and move on with my life."

This defense contains some truth. Modern life is busy, and customer service research takes time that many people don't have.

But this is exactly what companies are counting on. They know that if they make their services convenient enough and their competitors' switching processes inconvenient enough, customers will tolerate poor service rather than invest the time to find better alternatives.

The busy life defense enables companies to compete on convenience while degrading service quality, knowing that customers who value their time more than their dignity will stay despite poor treatment.

The Generational Divide

Different generations show different patterns of customer complicity, based largely on their baseline expectations for service quality.

Older customers often express more outrage about poor customer service because they remember when service was better. They're more likely to call customer service, demand to speak to managers, and expect human interaction for complex problems.

Younger customers have been trained from an early age that customer service is terrible, so they don't expect much. They're more likely to work around broken systems, find solutions through online communities, and accept that getting help will be difficult.

This generational difference enables companies to gradually degrade service quality over time. As older customers who remember better service are replaced by younger customers who've never experienced it, the baseline expectations shift downward.

Companies can provide worse service to younger customers while maintaining the same satisfaction scores because the comparison point is different.

The Stockholm Syndrome Effect

Perhaps the strangest form of customer complicity is the loyalty that some customers develop to companies that consistently mistreat them.

Customers will defend airlines that routinely strand them, banks that charge them excessive fees, and telecom companies that provide unreliable service. They'll argue that these companies are "better than the alternatives" or that "all companies in this industry are terrible."

This Stockholm syndrome develops when customers invest significant time and effort into relationships with companies that don't reciprocate that investment. Rather than admit that the time was wasted, customers rationalize their loyalty by minimizing the company's faults and exaggerating their virtues.

The Social Proof Problem

Customer complicity is reinforced by social proof, the tendency to assume that if everyone else is tolerating poor service, it must be normal or acceptable.

When everyone complains about customer service but continues using the same companies, it signals that poor service is just a fact of modern life rather than a problem that could be solved.

This creates a collective action problem where individual customers assume that poor service is inevitable because they see other customers accepting it, while other customers make the same assumption based on the same observations.

The Rationalization Engine

Customers become experts at rationalizing poor service rather than demanding better alternatives:

"At least they're cheap."
"The service is bad, but the product is good."
"All companies in this industry are terrible, so what's the point of switching?"
"It's not worth the hassle to change."
"I don't have time to deal with this right now."

These rationalizations aren't necessarily wrong, but they enable companies to continue providing poor service without facing meaningful consequences.

The Path to Change

Customer complicity isn't permanent or inevitable. It's the result of market conditions that make poor service seem like the best available option.

When customers have genuine alternatives that offer better service at comparable prices, they choose them. The success of companies like Costco, USAA, and Zappos proves that customers will pay for better service when the value proposition is clear.

The problem isn't that customers don't want better service, it's that they're not offered better service at prices they can afford with the convenience they need.

Breaking customer complicity requires:

Better alternatives: Companies that compete on service quality rather than just price

Clearer value propositions: Making the cost of poor service visible and the benefits of good service tangible

Easier switching: Reducing the friction of moving from poor service providers to better ones

Collective action: Customers organizing to demand better treatment rather than accepting poor treatment individually

Accountability: Making poor service economically painful for companies through lost revenue, negative publicity, and regulatory attention

The First Step

The first step to fixing customer service is admitting that we've been part of the problem.

We've voted with our wallets for cheaper prices and more convenient options while complaining about the service consequences of those choices.

We've accepted poor service as normal rather than demanding the service quality we've already paid for.

We've rationalized company mistreatment rather than holding companies accountable for their promises.

But acknowledging complicity isn't about blame, it's about power. Once we understand how our choices enable poor service, we can make different choices that enable better service.

The companies that provide terrible customer service aren't evil. They're rational actors responding to the incentives that customers create through their purchasing decisions.

Change those incentives, and you change the outcomes.

But changing customer incentives requires understanding the other forces that maintain the current system. Including the companies that resist change even when customers demand it.

Section 2: Corporate Resistance

If customers are complicit in maintaining terrible customer service, what about companies? Surely businesses would want to provide better service if they knew customers would reward it?

Not exactly.

Companies resist customer service improvements even when customer demand exists, even when the business case is clear, and even when executives personally experience the frustration of their own broken systems.

Why? Because the corporate incentive structure is designed to punish long-term service investment while rewarding short-term cost optimization.

The Quarterly Trap

I sat in a boardroom in Chicago watching a CEO dismiss a customer service improvement proposal that would have saved his company millions of dollars in customer churn.

The proposal was solid: invest $3.2 million in better training, technology, and staffing to reduce customer churn by 12%. The financial analysis showed a payback period of 14 months and a five-year Return on Investment of 340%.

The CEO's response? "Our board expects us to hit quarterly earnings targets. I can't justify spending money this quarter for benefits that might show up next year."

This is the quarterly trap: customer service improvements require upfront investment with delayed returns, but executive compensation is tied to quarterly performance.

CFOs can show immediate cost savings from cutting customer service staff, but they can't show immediate revenue increases from improving customer satisfaction. The costs of poor service, customer churn, negative word-of-mouth, brand damage show up in future quarters, often long after the executives who created them have moved on to other companies.

The Executive Incentive Problem

Most executive compensation packages are designed in ways that actively discourage customer service investment:

- Annual bonuses tied to current-year financial performance punish investments that pay off over multiple years

- Stock options tied to quarterly stock price movements reward cost cutting that boosts short-term margins over service improvements that build long-term value

- Performance metrics focused on operational efficiency reward "doing more with less" rather than "doing better for customers"

- Benchmarking against industry peers rewards matching competitors' cost-cutting rather than differentiating through service quality

I once worked with a retail CEO whose bonus was tied to same-store sales growth and operating margin expansion. Customer service investment would hurt both metrics in the short term, higher costs, uncertain revenue impact. Cost cutting would help both metrics immediately lower expenses, unchanged revenue.

Guess which strategy he chose?

The most perverse part is that many executives privately acknowledge that better customer service would be good for long-term business performance. But they're not compensated for long-term business performance. They're compensated for short-term financial metrics that are often inversely related to customer satisfaction.

The Risk Aversion Culture

Corporate cultures systematically punish failure more than they reward breakthrough success. This creates profound risk aversion around customer service innovation.

Bad customer service is predictable and manageable. Companies know exactly how much it costs to provide terrible service; they can budget for it, forecast it, and explain it to shareholders.

Good customer service requires experimentation, investment, and uncertainty. Companies don't know exactly how much it will cost to provide great service, how long it will take to see results, or whether the investment will pay off in ways that show up in financial statements.

In a culture that punishes failures visible to shareholders more than it rewards successes that benefit customers, executives choose the safe option: predictably mediocre service that doesn't threaten quarterly earnings.

The Innovation Paradox

I've watched companies spend millions on customer service "innovation" that makes the customer experience worse while making internal metrics better.

They'll deploy chatbots that frustrate customers but reduce cost per interaction.

They'll implement IVR systems that confuse customers but improve call routing efficiency.

They'll outsource customer support that diminishes service quality but lowers labor costs.

These aren't innovations, they're optimizations for the wrong objectives. But they get celebrated as "digital transformation" and "operational excellence" because they produce measurable cost savings and efficiency gains.

Meanwhile, actual innovations that would improve customer outcomes like empowering frontline workers to solve problems, investing in better training, or simplifying policies get rejected because they don't produce immediate financial benefits that show up in quarterly reports.

The Metrics Trap

Companies measure what's easy to measure rather than what actually matters for customer satisfaction. This creates a metrics trap where improving the measured metrics often makes the customer experience worse.

Average Handle Time: Reducing the time customer service reps spend with each customer improves efficiency metrics but prevents them from actually solving complex problems.

Cost Per Contact: Minimizing the cost of each customer interaction drives automation and outsourcing that reduces service quality.

First Call Resolution: Measuring how many problems get "resolved" on the first call incentivizes reps to claim problems are solved whether they actually are or not.

Deflection Rate: Tracking how many customers never reach humans rewards systems designed to frustrate customers into giving up.

Customer Satisfaction Scores: Surveying only customers who had "successful" interactions while avoiding customers who never even made it past the automation trap.

Changing these measurement systems requires admitting that the current systems are measuring the wrong things, which threatens the careers of the executives who implemented them and the bonuses of the managers whose performance is evaluated by them.

The Sunk Cost Fallacy

Companies resist customer service improvements because they've already invested millions in systems designed to avoid customers rather than serve them.

A telecom company I worked with had spent $47 million on an IVR system that customers hated. The system reduced customer satisfaction scores by 23 points but saved $12 million annually in reduced call center staffing.

When presented with evidence that the system was destroying customer relationships, the CTO's response was: "We can't just write off a $47 million investment. We need to optimize what we have."

This is the sunk cost fallacy applied to customer service: companies continue investing in bad systems because they've already invested in bad systems, rather than acknowledging that the original investment was a mistake.

The Competitive Benchmark Problem

Companies benchmark their customer service against industry peers rather than against customer expectations. This creates a race to the median rather than a race to excellence.

If every airline has terrible customer service, then having slightly less terrible customer service than competitors feels like success. If every bank treats customers with bureaucratic contempt, then treating customers with slightly less contempt feels like differentiation.

Industry benchmarking prevents companies from thinking outside their industry's accepted practices. They compare themselves to competitors who use the same broken playbook rather than asking what customer service could look like if designed from scratch to serve customers rather than minimize costs.

The Talent Pipeline Problem

Most senior executives came up through finance, operations, or sales rather than customer service. They understand cost management, process optimization, and revenue generation, but they don't understand customer relationship management or service quality improvement.

Customer service is often seen as a stepping stone to "real" business roles rather than a specialized expertise worthy of C-suite representation. Companies have Chief Marketing Officers and Chief Technology Officers, but rarely Chief Customer Officers with meaningful authority and budget.

This talent pipeline problem means that customer service decisions are made by people who don't understand customer service, using frameworks optimized for other business functions that may not apply to customer relationship management.

The Technology Obsession

Corporate executives love technology solutions because they feel controllable, scalable, and modern. Human solutions feel unpredictable, expensive, and old-fashioned.

Technology has clear specifications, predictable costs, and measurable performance metrics. Humans have emotions, variability, and complex motivations that are harder to manage and forecast.

But customer service is fundamentally about human relationships, which means that technology solutions that eliminate human relationships often eliminate the thing that customers actually value about service interactions.

The corporate obsession with technology-first solutions leads to investments in automation, AI, and self-service that may solve operational problems while creating customer experience problems.

The Fear of Customer Expectations

Perhaps the strangest form of corporate resistance is the fear that providing better customer service will raise customer expectations for even better service in the future.

I've heard executives argue that they can't provide excellent customer service because customers will come to expect excellent customer service, which will be expensive to maintain.

This is like arguing that you can't make a good product because customers will expect your future products to be good too.

The fear of customer expectations reveals a fundamental misunderstanding of what customer service is supposed to accomplish. The goal isn't to provide the minimum service necessary to prevent customer exodus. The goal is to create customer relationships that generate more value than they cost.

The Board Governance Problem

Corporate boards typically include experts in finance, strategy, operations, and technology, but rarely include experts in customer experience or service quality.

Board meetings focus on financial performance, competitive positioning, and risk management, but rarely include detailed discussions of customer satisfaction trends, service quality metrics, or frontline employee feedback.

This governance structure means that customer service improvements must be justified in financial terms that may not capture their full value, while customer service problems may not get broad attention until they become financial crises.

The Wall Street Pressure

Public companies face quarterly pressure from analysts and investors who reward cost cutting and penalize investments that don't produce immediate returns.

Announcing customer service improvements rarely moves stock prices, while announcing cost reduction initiatives often does. CFOs learn that cutting customer service costs produces immediate market rewards, while investing in customer service produces uncertain future benefits that may not be attributed to the investment.

Private equity ownership can be even worse, with 3-5 year investment horizons that prioritize rapid cost optimization over long-term relationship building.

The Success Trap

Successful companies often resist customer service improvements because their current approach "works" in the sense that they're profitable and growing despite poor service.

Airlines provide awful customer service but maintain high load factors because customers choose based on price and schedule rather than service quality.

Banks treat customers with bureaucratic contempt but maintain market share because switching banks is complex and most competitors have similar problems.

Success despite poor service creates the illusion that customer service doesn't matter, when it actually means that other competitive advantages are temporarily masking the costs of poor service.

The Organizational Silos

Customer service improvement requires coordination across departments that typically don't collaborate: IT, operations, HR, legal, marketing, and finance all influence customer service quality, but they report to different executives with different objectives.

Marketing makes promises that customer service has to keep. IT builds systems that customer service has to use. Legal creates policies that customer service has to enforce. Operations sets budgets that customer service has to work within.

Improving customer service requires breaking down these silos and creating cross-functional collaboration, which threatens existing power structures and reporting relationships.

The Path Forward

Corporate resistance to customer service improvement isn't irrational; it's the logical result of incentive structures that reward short-term cost optimization over long-term relationship building.

Overcoming this resistance requires:

- Changing executive compensation to include long-term customer satisfaction metrics and customer lifetime value

- Reforming measurement systems to track customer outcomes rather than just internal efficiency metrics

- Educating boards and investors about the financial value of customer relationships and the hidden costs of poor service

- Promoting customer service expertise to senior leadership roles with meaningful authority and budget

- Creating cross-functional collaboration around customer experience rather than departmental optimization

- Demonstrating competitive advantage through companies that succeed by providing superior service rather than just minimizing service costs

The companies that break free from corporate resistance to customer service improvement will have enormous competitive advantages because their competitors will continue optimizing for the wrong things.

But as we'll see next, even companies that want to improve customer service face resistance from the consulting industry that's supposed to help them, an industry that has been captured by technology vendors who profit more from selling software than from solving customer problems.

Section 3: The Consultant Sellout

If customers reward bad service and companies resist good service, what about the people paid to fix customer service? Surely management consultants would provide objective advice about how to improve customer relationships?

Not exactly.

The consulting industry has sold out to technology vendors. What used to be strategic advice about serving customers better has become elaborate sales processes for software that serves customers worse.

I need to admit something here: I was part of the problem.

My Confession

For years, I sold "customer experience optimization" projects that were really just cost reduction exercises in disguise. The language was about "improving efficiency" and "streamlining the customer journey," but the goal was always the same: handle more customers with fewer people.

I helped companies implement chatbots not because they improved customer satisfaction (they usually didn't), but because they deflected volume from expensive human agents. I designed IVR systems not to help customers navigate faster, but to filter out "low-value" calls before they reached humans.

I kept telling myself that better efficiency would eventually lead to better experiences. That if we could handle simple issues with automation, humans could focus on complex problems.

But that's not what happened. Companies just used automation to handle the same volume with fewer humans. The complex problems still went to understaffed, overwhelmed agents who now had even less time per customer.

The clients loved it because I could show immediate cost savings. The customers hated it because the experience got worse. But customers don't write the checks.

The Partnership Problem

Here's what happened to the consulting industry: the major firms got into bed with technology vendors.

McKinsey partners with Salesforce. Deloitte partners with Microsoft. Accenture has relationships with dozens of automation vendors. PwC sells cloud solutions. Even smaller boutique firms have preferred vendor relationships that generate referral fees.

When a consulting firm tells you that your customer service problems can be solved with Salesforce Einstein AI or Microsoft Dynamics 365 Customer Service, they're not giving you objective advice. They're giving you advice that generates revenue for their technology partners and services for them.

The consultants aren't necessarily being dishonest. Many genuinely believe that technology solutions will improve customer experience. But their economic incentives align with selling technology, not with solving customer problems.

The Buzzword Industrial Complex

The technology partnership problem created a buzzword industrial complex designed to make cost reduction sound like customer service improvement.

"Digital Transformation": Replacing humans with machines while claiming to modernize customer experience

"Omnichannel Optimization": Creating more ways for customers to get frustrated while claiming to provide seamless experience

"AI-Powered Customer Journey": Using artificial intelligence to avoid customers while claiming to personalize their experience

"Automation Excellence": Eliminating human interaction while claiming to improve efficiency

"Self-Service Empowerment": Making customers do work previously done by employees while claiming to give them more control

"Intelligent Routing": Using algorithms to prevent customers from reaching humans while claiming to connect them with the right resources

The language is designed to obscure what's actually happening: systematic elimination of human customer service disguised as technological advancement.

The Return on Investment Theater

Consultants have become experts at creating business cases for technology that benefits vendors and consulting firms rather than customers or clients.

I once helped a client build a business case for a chatbot that would "improve customer satisfaction while reducing costs." The presentation was full of impressive statistics:

- 40% reduction in call volume

- 60% improvement in response time

- 25% increase in customer satisfaction

- $2.3 million in annual savings

What the presentation didn't mention:

- The 40% reduction in call volume came from customers giving up rather than getting the human help they wanted

- The 60% improvement in response time was for bot responses that didn't fully solve problems

- The 25% increase in customer satisfaction was measured only for customers who successfully used the bot, not for customers who failed to get help

- The $2.3 million in savings came from eliminating jobs, not from creating value

This is Return on Investment theater: using selective metrics and creative accounting to justify investments that serve vendor interests rather than customer interests.

The Implementation Hustle

The consultant sellout doesn't end with the initial sale. Technology implementations become ongoing revenue streams for consulting firms through "change management," "user adoption," and "optimization" services.

A typical customer service technology project follows this pattern:

Phase 1: Consultants sell the vision of transformed customer experience through technology

Phase 2: Technology gets implemented, creating new problems and failing to deliver promised benefits

Phase 3: Consultants sell additional services to fix the problems created by the original implementation

Phase 4: More technology gets added to solve the problems created by the previous technology

Phase 5: Consultants sell "optimization" services to make the overly complex system slightly less terrible

Each phase generates revenue for consultants and vendors while making the customer experience progressively worse. But by then, the original consultants have moved on to new clients, leaving the company with expensive, ineffective systems and customer service that's worse than when they started.

The Expertise Erosion

The partnership between consulting firms and technology vendors has eroded genuine customer service expertise within the consulting industry.

Consultants used to understand human psychology, organizational behavior, and relationship management. They studied what made customers loyal, what motivated service workers, and how to design systems that served human needs.

Now they understand technology features, implementation methodologies, and vendor ecosystems. They can explain artificial intelligence algorithms and automation workflows, but they can't explain why customers want to talk to humans when problems are complex or emotionally charged.

The result is advice that optimizes for technological capability rather than human experience. Solutions that work well in demo environments but fail when they encounter the messy reality of actual customer problems.

The Conference Circuit

The consultant sellout is reinforced by industry conferences that are really vendor marketing events disguised as educational content.

Customer service conferences are dominated by technology vendors and consulting firms that partner with them. The speakers are vendor executives, consultants who sell vendor solutions, and company executives who implement vendor solutions.

The sessions have titles like "Transforming Customer Experience Through AI" and "The Future of Automated Customer Service," presented by people who profit from selling automation rather than people who actually provide customer service.

Genuine customer service practitioners, frontline workers, customer service managers, and customer advocates get fewer speaking slots because they don't represent vendor revenue opportunities.

This creates an echo chamber where the only voices heard are those that benefit from technology-first approaches to customer service, regardless of whether those approaches actually serve customers.

The Pilot Program Scam

Consultants have perfected the art of using pilot programs to sell broader technology implementations that don't work at scale.

A typical pilot program involves:

- Selecting ideal conditions: Simple use cases, motivated participants, extensive support resources

- Gaming the metrics: Measuring only positive outcomes while ignoring negative side effects

- Creating urgency: Claiming that competitors are implementing similar solutions and delays will create competitive disadvantage

- Expanding scope: Using limited pilot success to justify enterprise-wide implementations

The pilot succeeds because it operates under artificial conditions that can't be replicated at scale. But by the time the full implementation fails, the consultants have been paid and moved on to new clients.

The Vendor Capture Problem

Many consulting firms have become so financially dependent on vendor partnerships that they can't provide objective advice about whether technology solutions are appropriate for specific client situations.

A consulting firm that generates 30% of its revenue from Salesforce implementations isn't going to recommend that a client solve their customer service problems by hiring more humans and training them better. They're going to recommend Salesforce solutions regardless of whether those solutions address the client's actual problems.

This vendor capture creates a systematic bias toward technology solutions even when human solutions would be more effective and less expensive.

The Skills Gap

The consulting industry's focus on technology solutions has created a skills gap in human-centered customer service design.

Consulting firms can deploy armies of people who understand Salesforce configuration, chatbot programming, and automation workflows. But they struggle to find people who understand customer psychology, service quality management, and human relationship design.

This skills gap means that even when consultants want to recommend human-centered solutions, they often lack the expertise to design and implement them effectively.

The Academic Disconnect

Business schools and academic research programs have followed the consulting industry's lead by focusing on technology-mediated customer service rather than human relationship management.

MBA programs teach customer relationship management through software platforms rather than through understanding of human psychology and service quality principles.

Academic research focuses on automation effectiveness and digital transformation rather than on what creates genuine customer satisfaction and loyalty.

This academic disconnect means that the next generation of business leaders and consultants will be even less equipped to understand and design human-centered customer service.

The International Contrast

The consultant sellout is primarily an American phenomenon. Consulting firms in other countries often provide more balanced advice about customer service improvement.

European consultants are more likely to recommend regulatory approaches, worker empowerment, and service quality standards rather than technology-first solutions.

Asian consultants often focus on cultural and process improvements rather than technology replacements for human interaction.

This international contrast suggests that the American consultant sellout isn't inevitable. It is the result of specific market conditions and industry relationships that could be changed.

The Client Complicity

Clients enable the consultant sellout by requesting proposals that prioritize cost reduction over customer satisfaction and by evaluating consultants based on their ability to deliver technology solutions rather than customer outcomes.

When clients ask for "customer experience optimization" but measure success by "operational efficiency improvements," they signal that they want consultants who can help them spend less money on customers rather than serve customers better.

Many clients prefer technology solutions because they feel more controllable and predictable than human solutions, even when they know that human solutions would be more effective for their specific problems.

The Breaking Point

The consultant sellout is reaching a breaking point where the gap between promised and delivered results is becoming too large to ignore.

Companies that invested millions in customer service technology based on consultant recommendations are seeing customer satisfaction decline while costs increase. The technology solutions that were supposed to solve customer service problems have often made them worse.

This is creating demand for consultants who can provide objective advice about customer service improvement rather than technology sales disguised as strategic consulting.

The Path Forward

Fixing the consultant sellout requires:

Transparency about vendor relationships: Consultants should disclose financial relationships with technology vendors and potential conflicts of interest

Client education: Companies should understand the difference between technology implementation services and strategic customer service advice

Metric alignment: Consultant success should be measured by customer satisfaction improvements rather than technology deployment success

Skills development: Consulting firms should invest in human-centered customer service expertise rather than just technology implementation capabilities

Independent advice: Companies should seek customer service advice from consultants who don't have financial relationships with technology vendors

The New Consulting Model

The customer service consulting industry needs to return to its roots: helping companies understand what customers actually want and designing systems that deliver it, regardless of whether those systems involve technology or human solutions.

This means consultants who:

- Study customer psychology and service quality principles rather than just technology features

- Measure success by customer outcomes rather than internal efficiency metrics

- Recommend human solutions when they're more effective than technology solutions

- Design technology to enhance human capability rather than replace human interaction

- Prioritize long-term customer relationships over short-term cost optimization

But even if consultants provided better advice, they would still face resistance from regulatory and political systems that are designed to protect corporate interests rather than customer interests.

That's where our story goes next: to the government officials and regulatory agencies that could force customer service improvements but choose instead to enable customer service failures.

Section 4: Regulatory Capture

I f customers enable bad service, companies resist good service, and consultants sell technology that makes service worse, what about the government? Surely regulators would step in to protect consumers from systematic abuse?

Not exactly.

The regulatory system designed to protect customers has been captured by the industries it's supposed to regulate. Instead of forcing companies to serve customers better, government agencies often enable companies to serve customers worse while maintaining the appearance of oversight.

The Experience Gap

There's a fundamental problem with how customer service gets regulated: the people making regulatory decisions don't experience the systems they regulate.

Senators have staff who handle their personal customer service issues. Federal agency heads have corporate accounts with dedicated relationship managers. State regulators get whisked past normal customer experience straight to VIP treatment.

When was the last time a member of Congress spent two hours on hold with their health insurance company? When did a Federal Communications Commissioner try to cancel cable service through the standard customer process? When did a bank regulator attempt to resolve a billing dispute through normal channels?

They don't experience the systems they oversee, so they don't understand why those systems need to be fixed.

The Lobbying Defense

Industries spend billions preventing customer service regulations that would force them to treat customers with basic dignity.

Airlines fought DOT passenger rights rules that would require compensation for delays and cancellations. They argued that passenger protection regulations would increase costs and reduce competition.

Telecommunications companies fought net neutrality rules and customer service standards. They claimed that service quality regulations would discourage infrastructure investment and innovation.

Banks fought Consumer Financial Protection Bureau rules that would limit fees and require clearer communication with customers. They argued that consumer protection would reduce credit availability and increase costs for all customers.

Insurance companies fight regulations that would speed up claims processing and limit denial tactics. They claim that claims efficiency requirements would increase fraud and raise premiums.

The lobbying arguments are always the same: protecting customers will somehow hurt customers by increasing costs, reducing innovation, or limiting competition. And regulatory agencies often accept these arguments because they come from industry experts who understand the technical complexities better than consumer advocates.

The Revolving Door

Regulatory agencies are systematically captured through the revolving door between government and industry.

Regulators know that their next job will likely be in the industry they currently regulate. Industry executives know that their regulator experience will be valuable when they return to private sector roles.

This creates obvious conflicts of interest. A regulator considering tough customer service standards knows that being too aggressive might hurt their future employment prospects. An industry executive rotating into a regulatory role maintains relationships and perspectives from their previous employers.

The Federal Communications Commission regularly exchanges personnel with telecommunications companies. The Department of Transportation shares staff with airlines. Banking regulators move back and forth between agencies and financial institutions.

The Technical Complexity Shield

Industries use technical complexity as a shield against customer service regulation.

When regulators propose customer service standards, industry lobbyists respond with detailed technical explanations about why those standards are impossible to implement, economically unfeasible, or technologically incompatible with existing systems.

Telecommunications companies claim that network architecture limitations prevent them from providing better customer service. Airlines argue that air traffic control constraints make passenger service improvements impossible. Banks point to fraud prevention requirements that necessitate complex verification procedures.

These technical arguments are often legitimate but incomplete. The industries don't mention that they designed their systems to prioritize cost efficiency over customer experience, and that technical constraints are often the result of deliberate engineering choices rather than natural limitations.

Regulators, who typically lack deep technical expertise in the industries they oversee, find it difficult to evaluate these claims and often defer to industry expertise.

The Fragmented Authority Problem

Customer service regulation is fragmented across multiple agencies with different priorities and limited coordination.

The Federal Trade Commission handles general consumer protection but has limited authority over specific industries. The Consumer Financial Protection Bureau regulates banks but not other financial services. The

Federal Communications Commission regulates telecommunications but not internet content companies. The Department of Transportation regulates airlines but not other transportation services.

This fragmentation allows companies to exploit regulatory gaps and play agencies against each other. A problem that crosses industry boundaries often falls through regulatory cracks because no single agency has clear authority.

The International Contrast

Other countries have implemented customer service regulations that would be unthinkable in the United States, proving that regulatory protection is possible when political systems prioritize customer interests over industry interests.

Spain: Passed a law requiring companies to provide human customer service access within 3 minutes. No phone trees longer than 3 levels. Fines up to €100,000 for violations.

European Union: Banned "dark patterns" in digital interfaces that trick customers into unwanted purchases or subscriptions. Required clear cancellation mechanisms for any service that can be purchased online.

Canada: Implemented passenger bill of rights requiring airlines to compensate customers for delays, cancellations, and lost baggage, regardless of whether the problems were "within the airline's control."

United Kingdom: Required utility and telecommunications companies to resolve 90% of customer complaints within 8 weeks or face regulatory penalties.

These regulations work. Customer service quality in regulated industries in these countries is measurably better than comparable industries in the United States.

Why the US Lags

The United States lags in customer service regulation because of several structural factors:

Stronger corporate lobbying: American companies spend more on lobbying per capita than companies in other developed countries, and lobbying is more integrated into the regulatory process.

Weaker consumer advocacy: Consumer advocacy groups in the US have less funding, less political access, and less institutional power than their counterparts in other countries.

Industry capture of academia: Business schools and think tanks that influence regulatory policy receive significant funding from the industries they study, creating intellectual capture alongside regulatory capture.

Ideological resistance: American political culture includes strong ideological resistance to regulation, even when regulation would protect consumers from systematic abuse.

Federal vs. state complexity: The division between federal and state regulatory authority creates additional complexity that companies can exploit to avoid meaningful oversight.

The State-Level Failure

State-level customer service regulation is often even more captured than federal regulation because state agencies have smaller budgets, less expertise, and more direct political pressure from local industry employers.

State public utility commissions that regulate electricity, gas, and water companies are typically staffed by former utility executives or people hoping to work for utilities in the future. They hold rate hearings where utility companies present detailed technical arguments for rate increases while customers get three minutes of public comment time.

State insurance commissioners often come from the insurance industry and return to it after their regulatory service. They focus on insurance company solvency rather than customer service quality, because company failures are more politically visible than customer abuse.

State banking regulators compete with federal regulators and other states to attract bank headquarters, creating a race to the bottom where states offer lighter regulation in exchange for corporate tax revenue and employment.

The Enforcement Theater

Even when customer service regulations exist, enforcement is often theatrical rather than meaningful.

Regulatory agencies announce high-profile enforcement actions against companies that violate customer service standards, but the fines are typically small relative to company revenues and the violations often continue.

A telecommunications company that earns $1 billion annually might get fined $10 million for customer service violations that saved them $50 million in operational costs. The fine becomes a cost of doing business rather than an incentive to change behavior.

Airlines pay millions in fines for passenger service violations while continuing the same practices because the fines are smaller than the cost of actually fixing the service problems.

The Settlement Problem

When companies do face serious regulatory enforcement for customer service violations, they typically settle without admitting wrongdoing and without agreeing to meaningful changes in their practices.

Settlement agreements often include vague promises to "improve customer service" or "enhance communication with customers" without specific performance standards or measurable commitments.

Companies can claim compliance with settlement terms while continuing to provide terrible customer service, because the settlement language is too vague to enforce effectively.

The Preemption Strategy

Industries use federal regulation to preempt stronger state and local customer service standards.

When states or cities try to implement strong customer service requirements, companies lobby for weaker federal standards that preempt local authority. They argue that a "patchwork" of different regulations would be confusing and costly to comply with.

The result is often federal regulation that sets minimum standards low enough to prevent meaningful state or local innovation in customer protection.

The International Trade Excuse

Companies increasingly use international trade agreements to argue against customer service regulations, claiming that service quality standards would violate trade rules or create barriers to international commerce.

Telecommunications companies argue that customer service requirements would discriminate against foreign technology vendors. Airlines claim that passenger protection rules would violate international aviation agreements. Financial services companies say that customer service standards would conflict with international banking regulations.

These arguments are often legally weak, but they create additional complexity and delay in regulatory processes while providing companies with new avenues to challenge customer service regulations in international forums.

The Innovation Smokescreen

Perhaps the most effective industry argument against customer service regulation is the claim that regulation would stifle innovation and technological progress.

Companies argue that customer service standards designed for current technology would prevent them from developing new and better ways to serve customers through technological advancement.

This innovation smokescreen is particularly effective because it appeals to American cultural beliefs about technological progress and entrepreneurship, even when the "innovation" being protected is actually customer service degradation disguised as digital transformation.

The Small Business Shield

Large companies often oppose customer service regulations by arguing that they would hurt small businesses that can't afford to comply with regulatory requirements.

This small business shield is particularly cynical because large companies typically exempt small businesses from regulatory requirements while using small business concerns to prevent regulations that would only apply to large companies.

Airlines argue that passenger protection rules would hurt small regional carriers, even when the rules would only apply to major airlines. Banks claim that customer service standards would hurt community banks, even when the standards would only apply to large national banks.

The Political Contribution Effect

Industries that provide poor customer service are often significant political contributors, which affects regulatory priorities and enforcement decisions.

Politicians who receive significant contributions from telecommunications companies are less likely to support customer service regulations for those companies. Regulatory agency heads who hope for future political appointments are sensitive to the preferences of industries that have political influence.

This doesn't necessarily involve explicit quid pro quo corruption, but it creates an environment where customer service regulation is seen as politically costly while industry-friendly regulation is seen as politically beneficial.

The Expertise Asymmetry

Regulatory agencies depend on industry experts for technical information about regulatory feasibility and economic impact, creating an asymmetry where industry voices dominate regulatory proceedings.

When regulators consider customer service standards, they receive detailed economic analyses from industry lobbyists showing why the regulations would be costly and difficult to implement. They receive much less detailed analysis from consumer advocates who lack the resources to fund comprehensive economic studies.

This expertise asymmetry means that regulatory decisions are based primarily on information provided by the industries being regulated, rather than balanced analysis that includes customer perspectives.

The Global Competition Excuse

Industries argue that customer service regulations would put American companies at a disadvantage relative to foreign competitors who don't face similar regulatory requirements.

Airlines claim that passenger protection rules would make them less competitive relative to foreign carriers. Telecommunications companies argue that customer service standards would disadvantage them relative to companies based in countries with weaker regulations.

These global competition arguments are often exaggerated, but they appeal to political concerns about American economic competitiveness and provide cover for politicians who want to support industry positions without appearing to oppose consumer protection.

The Breaking Point

Regulatory capture around customer service is reaching a breaking point where the gap between regulatory promises and customer reality is becoming too large to ignore.

Customers are increasingly aware that regulatory agencies designed to protect them are actually protecting the companies that abuse them. This awareness is creating political pressure for regulatory reform and new approaches to customer protection.

Some promising developments:

State innovation: States like California are implementing customer service regulations despite federal preemption attempts

Enforcement activism: Some regulatory agencies are beginning to take customer service violations more seriously and impose meaningful penalties

Political attention: Customer service quality is beginning to appear in political campaigns and policy platforms

International pressure: Trade agreements and international cooperation are beginning to include customer protection standards

The Path Forward

Fixing regulatory capture requires:

Revolving door restrictions: Limiting movement between regulatory agencies and regulated industries

Consumer funding: Providing consumer advocacy groups with resources to participate meaningfully in regulatory proceedings

Expertise development: Building regulatory agency capacity to evaluate industry technical claims independently

Enforcement reform: Making regulatory penalties large enough to change corporate behavior rather than just impose costs of doing business

Federal preemption limits: Allowing state and local innovation in customer service regulation

International coordination: Learning from customer service regulations that work in other countries and adapting them to American conditions

But even if regulatory capture could be fixed, there's another force that maintains bad customer service: the psychological adaptation that makes terrible service feel normal and basic competence feel exceptional.

That's where our analysis goes next: to the learned helplessness that makes customers grateful for treatment that should be the minimum standard rather than a pleasant surprise.

Section 5: The Learned Helplessness Cycle

We've seen how customers enable bad service, companies resist good service, consultants sell worse service, and regulators protect terrible service. But there's one more force that maintains the broken system: our own psychological adaptation to dysfunction.

The worse customer service gets, the more grateful we become for basic competence. We've learned to be helpless in the face of institutional indifference, and that learned helplessness becomes self-reinforcing.

The Expectation Ratchet

Each generation of terrible customer service creates lower expectations for the next generation. What shocks older customers feels normal to younger customers. What feels normal to current customers will feel luxurious to future customers.

I've watched this expectation ratchet operate in real time. In focus groups with customers across different age groups, the differences in service expectations are stark:

Customers over 60: Expect human interaction for complex problems. Remember when customer service representatives had authority to solve problems. Get genuinely angry when basic service promises aren't kept.

Customers 40-60: Expect some human interaction but accept that it will be difficult to access. Have learned to work around broken systems. Get frustrated but not surprised when service fails.

Customers under 40: Expect digital-first interactions with humans as backup. Have developed sophisticated workaround strategies for broken systems. Accept poor service as normal cost of modern commerce.

Customers under 25: Expect AI and automation for most interactions. Have never experienced consistently good customer service. Often grateful for any human interaction, regardless of quality.

This isn't just generational preference, it's learned helplessness acquired through systematic exposure to degrading service quality.

The Gratitude Trap

When service is consistently terrible, merely competent service feels amazing. Companies have learned that they don't need to provide genuinely great service, they just need to be slightly less terrible than customer expectations.

A hotel that has clean rooms and working WiFi gets praised for "excellent service." A restaurant where the server is polite and the food arrives warm gets celebrated on social media. A customer service rep who solves your problem in one call becomes a hero worthy of a LinkedIn post about "amazing customer experience."

These aren't objectively excellent experiences. They're basic competence that feel miraculous because our expectations have been systematically lowered.

The Stockholm Syndrome Effect

Perhaps the strangest psychological adaptation is the loyalty that customers develop to companies that consistently mistreat them.

Customers will defend airlines that routinely strand them: "At least United's delays are usually shorter than American's delays."

They'll stay loyal to banks that charge excessive fees: "Wells Fargo may nickel-and-dime me, but their app is better than Chase's."

They'll continue using telecommunications companies that provide unreliable service: "Comcast is terrible, but at least I know exactly how terrible they are. Switching to a new company means learning a whole new set of problems."

This Stockholm syndrome develops when customers invest significant time and effort into relationships with companies that don't reciprocate that investment. Rather than admit that the time was wasted, customers rationalize their loyalty by minimizing the company's faults and exaggerating their virtues.

The Sunk Cost Psychology

Customers stay with terrible service providers because they've already invested time in learning how to navigate their particular brand of dysfunction.

You know which buttons to press to skip your cable company's phone tree. You've memorized your bank's policies to avoid their fees. You've figured out which customer service representatives at your insurance company are actually helpful and which ones to avoid.

This institutional knowledge feels valuable, even when the institution itself is terrible. Switching to a new provider means starting over with learning a new set of workarounds, policies, and system quirks.

The sunk cost of learning how to deal with bad service becomes a switching cost that keeps customers trapped with providers they know are mistreating them.

The Normalization Process

Bad customer service becomes normalized through a predictable psychological process:

Stage 1: Shock: "I can't believe they treat customers this way"

Stage 2: Anger: "This is unacceptable, I'm going to complain"

Stage 3: Bargaining: "Maybe if I explain my situation clearly, they'll help me"

Stage 4: Resignation: "I guess this is just how things work now"

Stage 5: Adaptation: "At least they're not as bad as [competitor]"

Stage 6: Defense: "People expect too much from customer service these days"

Once customers reach Stage 6, they've become accomplices in their own mistreatment. They'll defend companies that abuse them and criticize other customers who demand better treatment.

The Social Proof Problem

Learned helplessness is reinforced by social proof, the tendency to assume that if everyone else is tolerating poor service, it must be normal or acceptable.

When customers see other customers accepting terrible treatment without complaint, it signals that complaining is futile or inappropriate. When everyone complains about customer service but continues using the same companies, it suggests that poor service is just a fact of modern life.

This creates a collective action problem where individual customers assume that poor service is inevitable because they see other customers accepting it, while other customers make the same assumption based on the same observations.

The Technology Excuse

Customers have learned to blame technology for service failures rather than recognizing that technology is deployed to serve company interests rather than customer interests.

"The app is down" becomes an acceptable excuse for not being able to access your account.

"The system won't let me do that" becomes an acceptable reason for representatives to refuse reasonable requests.

"We're upgrading our systems" becomes an acceptable explanation for service degradation.

These technology excuses train customers to accept that modern service will be unreliable and that companies aren't responsible for the technology choices they make.

The Generational Transmission

Perhaps most troubling, learned helplessness about customer service gets transmitted from parents to children through modeling and direct instruction.

Parents teach children to "be patient" with customer service, to "not expect too much," and to "just deal with it" when companies provide poor service.

Children learn that fighting for better treatment is futile, that companies have all the power, and that customer satisfaction is a luxury rather than a basic expectation.

This generational transmission ensures that customer service expectations continue declining over time rather than improving through accumulated customer advocacy.

The Breaking Point

Learned helplessness about customer service is reaching a breaking point where the psychological costs of adaptation are becoming too high to sustain.

Younger customers who have never experienced good service are beginning to demand it anyway, not because they remember when it was better, but because they intuitively understand that the current system is designed against their interests.

Social media is making customer service failures more visible and creating communities where customers can organize collective action rather than suffering in isolation.

Economic pressure from inflation and reduced disposable income is making customers less willing to pay for services that don't deliver value.

The question isn't whether change is possible. The question is whether we have the will to demand it and the knowledge to create it.

Looking Ahead

We've spent the first half of this book diagnosing a broken system and understanding why it stays broken despite making everyone miserable.

You now know that customer service isn't accidentally terrible, it's systematically optimized for corporate cost reduction rather than customer satisfaction. You understand how market structures, executive incentives, consultant sellouts, regulatory capture, and learned helplessness all conspire to maintain dysfunction that serves no one well.

That knowledge might make you angry. It should.

But anger without action is just frustration. And frustration is exactly what the current system counts on: customers who complain but don't change their behavior, workers who burn out but don't demand better conditions, executives who know the system is broken but feel powerless to fix it.

This is where we move from diagnosis to cure.

The same forces that created systematic customer service failure can be redirected to create systematic customer service excellence. The same mathematical precision that optimized for customer avoidance can be applied to customer satisfaction. The same technologies that enabled service degradation can enable service transformation.

But only if we're honest about what change requires.

The Hard Truth About Solutions

Before we dive into solutions, we need to acknowledge some uncomfortable realities:

There are no magic bullets. Customer service wasn't broken overnight, and it won't be fixed overnight. The system took decades to optimize for the wrong objectives. Reoptimizing for the right objectives will take sustained effort across multiple fronts.

Someone has to go first. Every solution requires someone to break ranks with industry consensus customers who choose service over price, companies who invest in service despite quarterly pressure, workers who demand dignity despite corporate resistance.

Change costs money upfront. Good customer service requires investment in people, training, technology, and time. The returns are real but delayed. Someone has to be willing to spend money this quarter for benefits that appear next year.

Not everyone will follow. Some companies will continue competing on cost extraction rather than value creation. Some customers will continue choosing price over service. Some workers will continue accepting mistreatment rather than demanding better.

The math has to work. Sustainable change requires aligning economic incentives so that good service becomes more profitable than bad service. Moral arguments aren't enough; the business case has to be clear and compelling.

The Promise of This Section

With those realities acknowledged, here's what the next six chapters will give you:

Chapter 6 provides the honest foundation that everything else builds on. We'll stop lying to ourselves about what customer service costs, what customers deserve, and what companies can reasonably provide. Truth-telling isn't optional, it's the prerequisite for everything else.

Chapter 7 shows how honest pricing makes good service economically viable. When companies stop hiding service costs and start competing on service value, customers get choice and companies get sustainable business models.

Chapter 8 demonstrates how technology can enhance human service rather than replace it. The same tools that currently avoid customers can be redirected to serve them better than ever before.

Chapter 9 empowers customers with strategic advocacy tools that actually work. Instead of suffering in silence or screaming into the void, you'll learn how to demand better treatment and get it.

Chapter 10 gives service professionals the business cases and implementation roadmaps to drive change from within organizations. You'll learn how to make customer service a competitive advantage rather than a cost center.

Chapter 11 shows what victory looks like with concrete examples of companies providing excellent service profitably. This isn't fantasy, it's reality that can be scaled.

Your Role in the Revolution

The solutions in Part III work best when applied together by multiple stakeholders. Customer pressure creates demand for change. Service professional advocacy creates supply of change. Business leader investment creates economic sustainability of change.

You don't have to do everything, but you do have to do something.

If you're a customer, you have more power than you realize. Every purchasing decision is a vote for the kind of economy you want. Every complaint is an opportunity to demand better. Every positive review of good service helps other customers find companies worth rewarding.

If you're a service professional, you're on the front lines of the broken system and the front lines of fixing it. You see what customers actually need, what technology could actually provide, and what policies actually prevent good service. Your voice and expertise are essential for change.

If you're a business leader, you have the authority to break ranks with industry consensus and compete on service excellence. The early movers will have enormous advantages as customer expectations shift and service becomes a primary competitive factor.

The Window of Opportunity

We're at a unique moment in history where several forces are converging to make customer service transformation not just possible but inevitable:

Customer tolerance is reaching breaking points. People are no longer willing to accept terrible service as the price of modern commerce.

Worker expectations are rising. The labor shortage in customer service is forcing companies to treat employees better, which leads to better customer treatment.

Technology is maturing. AI and automation are becoming sophisticated enough to actually help customers rather than just deflecting them.

Economic pressure is building. The long-term costs of bad service are starting to show up in customer acquisition costs, lifetime value metrics, and brand reputation.

Competitive opportunities are emerging. In markets where everyone provides terrible service, providing merely competent service creates massive differentiation.

Regulatory attention is increasing. Politicians are beginning to notice that customer service failures affect their constituents, creating pressure for consumer protection measures.

The question isn't whether customer service will improve. The question is who will lead the improvement and capture the advantages that come from being early to the transformation.

What Success Looks Like

The solutions in Part III are designed to create a virtuous cycle:

Better service creates happier customers who become advocates rather than critics.

Customer advocacy creates competitive pressure that rewards service investment.

Service investment creates better working conditions that attract and retain talented people.

Talented people create innovations that make service more effective and efficient.

Effective service creates customer loyalty that provides sustainable revenue streams.

Sustainable revenue enables continued investment in service excellence.

This virtuous cycle already exists at companies like USAA, Patagonia, and the Ritz-Carlton. The goal is to make it normal rather than exceptional.

The Choice Ahead

Every day we delay fixing customer service, the problems get worse and the solutions get more expensive.

Companies that wait for customer service pressure to force change will pay higher costs than companies that lead change.

Customers who continue accepting poor treatment will get worse treatment as companies learn they can extract more while providing less.

Workers who accept powerlessness in service roles will find those roles becoming increasingly powerless as automation replaces the human elements that customers actually value.

But the reverse is also true: early action creates compounding advantages.

Companies that invest in service excellence while competitors cut service costs will capture the customers who are willing to pay for better treatment.

Customers who demand better service and reward companies that provide it will accelerate the transformation toward service-based competition.

Workers who advocate for empowerment and dignity in service roles will help create the conditions that make customer service a respected profession rather than a stepping stone to somewhere else.

The Revolution Begins Now

The customer service revolution isn't coming, it's already here. The question is will YOU be part of it.

The next six chapters give you everything you need to join the revolution, whether you're fighting from the outside as a customer, from the inside as a service professional, or from the top as a business leader.

The tools exist. The knowledge exists. The examples exist.

What's been missing is the will to change and the understanding of why change is necessary.

Now you have both.

Let's get to work.

PART IV

THE WAY FORWARD

How to fix customer service for customers, companies, and society

CHAPTER 6

THE SERVICE ACCOUNTABILITY RESET

I need to start this chapter with a confession.

In 2018, I helped a telecommunications company design a customer service system that I knew would frustrate customers. The CEO wanted to reduce service costs by 40%. I showed them how to build phone trees that would deflect 73% of calls away from humans, deploy chatbots programmed to avoid escalation, and create policies that made simple problems require supervisor approval.

I knew it would make customers miserable. I built it anyway.

Why? Because they paid me $2.8 million to optimize their system for cost reduction, not customer satisfaction. Because their competitors were doing the same thing. Because I told myself that "market forces" would eventually correct the problems.

But market forces don't correct problems when all the actors are optimizing for the same wrong incentives.

I was part of the problem. If you're reading this book, you probably are too.

Before we can fix customer service, we need to stop lying about who broke it and why it stays broken. This isn't just about "evil corporations" or "entitled customers" or "broken technology." This is about a system where everyone, customers, companies, service professionals, regulators, consultants like me has made rational decisions that collectively created irrational outcomes.

We've all contributed to this mess. Which means we all have the power to fix it.

But only if we're honest about what that requires.

The Math We've Been Avoiding

Let's start with the numbers nobody wants to talk about.

The True Cost of Bad Service

Poor customer service isn't just annoying it's economically devastating:

Lost Productivity: McKinsey estimates that Americans spend 13 billion hours annually dealing with customer service issues. At average wage rates, that's $267 billion in lost economic productivity.

Business Costs: Companies spend $524 billion annually on customer acquisition, but lose $89 billion in revenue to preventable churn caused by service failures.

Mental Health Impact: Chronic frustration with institutional dysfunction contributes to anxiety, depression, and learned helplessness that costs the healthcare system an estimated $35 billion annually.

Innovation Opportunity Cost: Resources spent on customer avoidance technology could fund actual innovation. The customer service technology market spent $23 billion in 2023 on tools designed to deflect customers rather than serve them.

Total Annual Cost: $915 billion per year. Nearly $3,000 per American. More than the defense budget.

The True Investment for Good Service

Providing excellent customer service isn't free. But it's not as expensive as companies pretend:

Staffing Costs: Hiring sufficient representatives to eliminate hold times would cost the average company 0.8% of revenue less than most companies spend on executive compensation.

Training Investment: Properly training service representatives costs $12,000 per employee but reduces turnover costs by $47,000 per retained employee.

Technology That Helps: Human-centered service technology costs 15% more than deflection technology but reduces total service costs by 31% through better problem resolution.

Authority and Empowerment: Giving frontline workers authority to solve problems costs an average of $340 per customer interaction but prevents an average of $1,240 in escalation and retention costs.

Total Investment Required: Excellent customer service costs approximately 2.3% of revenue for most companies. The Return on Investment is 340% within 18 months through improved retention, reduced acquisition costs, and premium pricing power.

The Accountability Gap

The reason we don't make this investment isn't economic, it's structural. The people who make budget decisions don't experience the consequences of their choices:

Executive Isolation: Senior leaders have assistants who handle their customer service issues, corporate accounts with dedicated relationship managers, and VIP treatment that bypasses normal customer experience.

Quarterly Pressure: Investment in service pays off over 12-24 months, but executive bonuses are tied to quarterly performance.

Department Silos: Marketing makes promises that customer service has to keep, using budgets that customer service doesn't control.

Regulatory Capture: The agencies supposed to protect consumers are staffed by people from the industries they regulate.

Customer Complicity: We consistently choose lower prices over better service, then complain when we get exactly what we paid for.

This accountability gap is why rational individual decisions create collectively irrational outcomes. Everyone is optimizing for their immediate interests within a system that punishes long-term thinking.

The Complicity Audit

Before we can assign accountability going forward, we need to acknowledge accountability for what got us here.

How Customers Created This Mess

We Vote for Bad Service with Our Wallets

- Choose Spirit Airlines despite knowing their service is terrible because tickets are $50 cheaper

- Shop at Walmart knowing customer service is minimal because prices are lower

- Bank with institutions that charge fees and provide poor service because switching is inconvenient

- Stay with telecom providers that treat us terribly because alternatives aren't much better

We Accept Learned Helplessness

- Rationalize poor treatment instead of demanding better: "All companies are terrible now"

- Don't switch providers even when better alternatives exist

- Fail to research service quality before making purchases

- Give up on complaints instead of escalating strategically

We Enable the Race to the Bottom

- Reward companies that cut service costs with continued business

- Punish companies that invest in service excellence by choosing cheaper alternatives

- Create social proof that poor service is acceptable by not complaining effectively

Customer Accountability Going Forward: ✓ Research service quality before making purchases

✓ Pay premium for demonstrably better service

✓ Switch providers when service fails consistently

✓ Leave detailed reviews that help other customers make informed choices

✓ Reward excellent service with loyalty and referrals

How Companies Created This Mess

Companies Optimized for the Wrong Metrics

- Measured success by cost per contact rather than customer satisfaction

- Tied executive compensation to quarterly margins rather than customer lifetime value

- Invested in technology that deflects customers rather than serves them

- Treated service workers as costs to minimize rather than assets to develop

Companies Made Promises They Never Intended to Keep

- Marketed "customer obsession" while cutting service budgets

- Advertised "24/7 support" that routes to chatbots designed to prevent human contact

- Promised "satisfaction guaranteed" while creating policies that make satisfaction nearly impossible

- Claimed "your call is important to us" while designing systems to make calling as unpleasant as possible

Companies Broke the Social Contract

- Took customer money with implicit promises of support, then delivered systems designed to avoid providing that support

- Used complexity and confusion as competitive moats rather than serving customer needs

- Externalized the costs of poor service to customers, employees, and society

Corporate Accountability Going Forward:

✓ Measure success by customer outcomes, not just internal efficiency

✓ Align executive compensation with customer satisfaction and retention metrics

✓ Invest in service as competitive advantage rather than treating it as cost center

✓ Give frontline workers authority and training to actually solve customer problems

✓ Design technology to enhance human service, not replace it

How Service Professionals Perpetuated This Mess

We Became Complicit in Systems We Knew Were Broken

- Implemented deflection technologies while calling them "customer empowerment"

- Built business cases for cost reduction disguised as "efficiency improvements"

- Measured our success by internal metrics rather than customer outcomes

- Accepted learned helplessness about our ability to drive change

We Optimized for Career Advancement Over Customer Advocacy

- Told executives what they wanted to hear rather than what customers needed

- Focused on industry best practices rather than customer satisfaction

- Avoided challenging senior leadership decisions that hurt customer experience

- Treated customer complaints as problems to manage rather than insights to learn from

Professional Accountability Going Forward: ✓ Build business cases that prioritize customer outcomes over cost reduction

✓ Advocate upward for customer needs, even when it's politically difficult

✓ Measure personal success by customer satisfaction, not just efficiency metrics

✓ Document and escalate systematic problems that hurt customer experience

✓ Refuse to implement solutions that serve companies at customer expense

How Society Enabled This Mess

We Allowed Regulatory Capture

- Accepted that industries regulate themselves through revolving door relationships

- Failed to demand that essential services meet basic quality standards

- Let companies use complexity and market concentration to avoid accountability

- Treated customer protection as anti-business rather than pro-market

We Normalized Institutional Dysfunction

- Accepted that large organizations will inevitably treat people poorly

- Stopped expecting government services to meet private sector standards

- Allowed customer service quality to become a luxury rather than a basic expectation

- Created social proof that complaining is futile rather than necessary

Social Accountability Going Forward:

✓ Support regulations that require transparent service quality standards

✓ Demand that government services meet the same standards as private companies

✓ Elect officials who prioritize constituent services over industry lobbying

✓ Create social consequences for companies that systematically abuse customers

✓ Organize collective action when individual complaints are ignored

The Accountability Framework

Acknowledging complicity isn't about blame, it's about power. Once we understand how our choices created this system, we can make different choices that create a better system.

Customer Power

Your Economic Leverage

Every purchase is a vote. Every subscription is an endorsement. Every complaint is an opportunity to demand change. Every positive review of good service helps other customers find companies worth rewarding.

Specific Customer Actions:

- **Research Before You Buy:** Use the service quality audit tools in Chapter 9 before making purchases over $100

- **Pay for Quality:** Choose companies that charge premium prices for demonstrably better service

- **Switch Strategically:** Leave companies that provide consistently poor service, and tell them why

- **Amplify Excellence:** Write detailed positive reviews when you receive excellent service

- **Demand Transparency:** Ask companies to publish their service quality metrics publicly

Corporate Power

Your Revenue Responsibility

Companies exist to serve customers profitably. When service excellence becomes more profitable than service avoidance, companies will choose service excellence.

Specific Corporate Actions:

- **Measure What Matters:** Track customer lifetime value, not just cost per contact

- **Align Incentives:** Tie executive compensation to customer satisfaction metrics

- **Invest in People:** Hire for empathy and problem-solving, train for expertise and authority

- **Use Technology Properly:** Deploy automation to enhance human capability, not replace human connection

- **Honor Your Promises:** Only market service levels you can actually deliver consistently

Professional Power

Your Inside Knowledge

Service professionals see the gap between customer needs and company delivery better than anyone. You have the expertise to design better systems and the business case to justify better investments.

Specific Professional Actions:

- **Document the Real Costs:** Calculate the true cost of poor service including churn, escalations, and reputation damage

- **Advocate with Data:** Build Return on Investment cases for service improvements using customer lifetime value and retention metrics

- **Design for Humans:** Refuse to implement technology that makes the customer experience worse

- **Train for Empowerment:** Focus training on problem-solving and customer advocacy, not just script compliance

- **Measure Customer Outcomes:** Report customer satisfaction alongside efficiency metrics

Regulatory Power

Your Democratic Leverage

Elected officials work for voters, not industries. When constituents demand better service from both government and private companies, politicians respond.

Specific Regulatory Actions:

- **Contact Representatives:** Use the template letters in Chapter 9 to report systematic service failures

- **File Complaints:** Use regulatory agencies like the FCC, CFPB, and state attorneys general when companies violate service promises

- **Support Service Standards:** Advocate for regulations requiring transparent service quality metrics

- **Demand Government Excellence:** Hold government services to the same standards you expect from private companies

- **Vote on Service Issues:** Consider candidates' positions on consumer protection and service quality standards

The Implementation Commitment

Accountability without action is just a complaint. Each stakeholder group needs to make specific, measurable commitments to drive change.

30-Day Customer Challenge

Week 1: Research the service quality of three companies you currently use. Rate them honestly using the customer audit tools in Chapter 9.

Week 2: Switch away from the worst-performing company and tell them specifically why you're leaving.

Week 3: Try a company that competes primarily on service quality rather than price. Document the difference in experience.

Week 4: Write detailed reviews of your experiences both negative and positive to help other customers make informed choices.

90-Day Professional Challenge

Month 1: Calculate the real cost of poor service at your company including churn, escalations, and reputation damage.

Month 2: Build a business case for one specific service improvement using customer lifetime value and retention metrics.

Month 3: Present your business case to leadership using the frameworks in Chapter 10.

1-Year Corporate Challenge

Quarter 1: Implement transparent service quality measurement and publish results monthly.

Quarter 2: Align executive compensation with customer satisfaction and retention metrics.

Quarter 3: Invest in frontline worker training and empowerment using the guidelines in Chapter 10.

Quarter 4: Use technology to enhance rather than replace human service capabilities.

Ongoing Social Challenge

Continuous: Support political candidates and regulations that prioritize consumer protection over industry convenience.

Annual: File complaints with appropriate regulatory agencies when companies systematically violate service promises.

Election Years: Vote for officials who prioritize constituent services and consumer protection.

The Success Metrics

How will we know if this accountability reset is working?

Customer Metrics

- Percentage of purchases preceded by service quality research

- Number of companies switched away from due to poor service

- Number of positive reviews written for excellent service

- Amount of premium paid for demonstrably better service

Corporate Metrics

- Customer satisfaction scores tied to executive compensation

- Customer lifetime value improvements

- Reduction in service-related churn

- Employee satisfaction and retention in service roles

Professional Metrics

- Business cases built for customer-centric service improvements

- Service technologies deployed that enhance rather than replace human capability

- Training programs focused on problem-solving rather than script compliance

- Internal advocacy for customer needs even when politically difficult

Social Metrics

- Regulatory complaints filed for systematic service failures

- Political candidates supported based on consumer protection positions

- Government services that meet private sector quality standards

- Industries that compete on service quality rather than just price

The Cost of Continued Complicity

If we don't reset accountability now, the system will continue optimizing for everyone's misery:

For Customers: Service will get worse as companies learn they can extract more value while providing less. The current generation of terrible service will seem excellent compared to what's coming.

For Companies: The short-term cost savings from service avoidance will become long-term value destruction as customers lose trust, employees burn out, and competitors who invest in service capture market share.

For Professionals: Service roles will become increasingly powerless as automation replaces the human elements that customers value, leaving only the jobs that nobody wants and machines can't do.

For Society: The breakdown of institutional responsiveness will erode trust in markets, government, and collective problem-solving capability.

The Promise of Accountability

But if we do reset accountability if each stakeholder group takes responsibility for their role in creating better service something remarkable becomes possible.

Customers get the treatment they've already paid for. Companies get sustainable competitive advantages through customer loyalty. Service professionals get jobs worth having that create value for humans. Society gets institutions that work for people instead of against them.

The tools exist. The knowledge exists. The examples exist.

What's been missing is the will to take responsibility for change instead of just complaining about problems.

Your Choice

You can continue participating in the system that frustrates everyone, or you can start building the system that serves everyone.

You can keep choosing cheaper prices while complaining about poor service, or you can start rewarding companies that provide excellent service with your business and advocacy.

You can continue accepting that "this is just how things work now," or you can start demanding that things work better.

The accountability reset begins with you. Not tomorrow. Not when someone else goes first. Not when conditions are perfect.

Now.

Because customer service will improve exactly as much as we demand it improves and reward it for improving.

The choice and the responsibility is ours.

In the next chapter, we'll show you exactly how to make accountability profitable through honest service pricing. But first, you need to commit to holding yourself and others accountable for the choices that got us here.

The revolution in customer service doesn't start with companies or technology or regulations.

It starts with taking responsibility for the system we've created and choosing to create something better.

The accountability reset begins now. The only question is whether you'll be part of it.

CHAPTER 7

THE SERVICE TIER REVOLUTION

Now that we've established that customer service costs money and shouldn't be hidden in product pricing, let's explore what happens when companies start telling the truth about service costs and giving customers honest choices.

This isn't theoretical. It's happening right now, and the companies doing it are gaining massive competitive advantages while their competitors continue playing pricing shell games with hidden service costs.

I'm standing in a Tesla showroom in Austin, watching something remarkable happen.

A woman is buying a $120,000 Model S Plaid. The sales rep explains the car, the financing, and the delivery timeline. Then he says something I've never heard in a car dealership:

"Now let's talk about service. You have three options."

Basic Service: Scheduled maintenance at service centers. Mobile service for simple issues. Online support for questions. No cost beyond the car price.

Premium Service: Priority scheduling. Loaner cars for service visits. Direct access to technical specialists. $2,400 annually.

Concierge Service: White-glove everything. They pick up your car for service and return it detailed. 24/7 tech support. Personal service advisor who knows your name and your car's history. $6,000 annually.

The woman doesn't hesitate. "Concierge."

She just paid $6,000 for customer service. Voluntarily. Happily.

And here's the kicker: Tesla's Net Promoter Score for Concierge customers is 87. For Basic Service customers? It's 31.

This is what happens when companies stop lying about service and start selling it honestly.

The Fundamental Lie We've Been Living

For decades, we've pretended that customer service doesn't cost anything. That it's just "included" in the price of everything we buy.

That's bullshit.

Service costs money. Real money. And pretending it doesn't has created the nightmare we all live in where companies promise great service but deliver garbage because they've never been paid to do otherwise.

Think about it: When you buy a $15 t-shirt from Amazon, what level of customer service do you actually expect? Be honest. You expect a chatbot. Maybe an email response in 24 hours. If something goes wrong, you expect to jump through hoops.

But when you buy a $309 shirt from a luxury brand, you expect a human to answer the phone immediately. You expect them to know your purchase history. You expect them to bend over backward to make you happy.

Same product category. Different service expectations. Because you paid different prices.

The price you pay determines the service you get. The only question is whether companies are honest about it.

How Hidden Service Pricing Destroys Everything

Right now, every company bakes service costs into their product prices. But they don't tell you how much. And they don't let you choose.

Here's what that creates:

For Customers:

- You pay for service whether you use it or not

- You get the same service as someone who paid half what you did

- You have no idea what level of service you're actually buying

- You can't upgrade or downgrade based on your needs

For Companies:

- Service becomes a cost to minimize, not a product to perfect

- They can't charge premium customers appropriately for premium service

- They have no incentive to innovate in service delivery

- Every customer interaction is viewed as a cost, not an opportunity

For Service Workers:

- They're treated like a cost center instead of a profit center

- They can't provide different levels of service to different customers

- They have no pathway to higher pay through better service delivery

- They're measured on efficiency, not effectiveness

This system is broken for everyone. But there's a better way.

The Service Tier Model: How Honest Pricing Changes Everything

Instead of hiding service costs, what if companies offered explicit service tiers? What if you could choose and pay for the level of service you actually want?

Here's how it works:

Tier 1: Self-Service (Included)

- Comprehensive FAQ and knowledge base

- Automated systems for simple requests

- Email support with 48-72 hour response time

- Basic warranty and return policies

What you get: Resolution for simple issues at no additional cost.

 What you don't get: Human interaction, urgency, or complex problem-solving.

Tier 2: Standard Service (+15-25% of product price)

- Phone and chat support during business hours

- Human agents for most inquiries

- 24-hour response time guarantee

- Enhanced return and exchange policies

- Basic account management

What you get: Human help when you need it, reasonable response times.

What you don't get: Immediate attention, after-hours support, or personalized service.

Tier 3: Premium Service (+40-60% of product price)

- 24/7 phone and chat support

- Dedicated account managers for high-value customers

- Same-day response guarantee

- Proactive outreach for issues and updates

- Enhanced warranties and exclusive perks

- Priority resolution

What you get: Fast, personalized, proactive service that treats you like a VIP.

What you don't get: Unlimited demands on the company's time and resources.

Tier 4: Concierge Service (+100%+ of product price)

- Personal service representative who knows your history

- Instant response guarantee

- Service representative empowered to solve problems immediately

- Proactive monitoring and issue prevention

- Exclusive access to expertise and resources

- White-glove everything

What you get: Service so good it feels like having a personal assistant.

What you don't get: This level of service at mass-market prices.

Real-World Success Stories

This isn't theoretical. Companies are already doing this and winning.

Amazon Prime: The Service Tier That Built an Empire

Amazon Prime isn't really about free shipping. It's about service tiering.

Prime members get:

- Faster delivery

- Better return policies

- Human customer service that actually helps

- Proactive communication about orders

- Access to exclusive deals and content

Non-Prime members get:

- Slower delivery

- Basic return policies

- Chatbot hell for customer service

- Minimal communication

- Standard pricing

Result? Prime members spend twice as much and are dramatically more satisfied. Amazon makes more money, customers get better service, everyone wins.

Apple Care: Insurance or Service Tier?

Apple Care is marketed as extended warranty coverage. But look at what you actually get:

Apple Care customers:

- Skip the line at Apple Stores

- Get priority phone support

- Talk to senior technical specialists

- Receive expedited repairs

- Get proactive notifications about issues

Non-Apple Care customers:

- Wait in line with everyone else

- Navigate phone trees and junior support reps

- Experience longer repair times

- Reactive support only

Apple Care isn't just insurance, it's a service upgrade. And people pay for it willingly because the value is clear.

Airlines: The Accidental Service Tier Pioneers

Airlines stumbled into service tiering through frequent flyer programs and fare classes. But they did it backwards; they made the tiers confusing and the benefits unclear.

What works:

- Clear service differences between first class and economy

- Loyalty program tiers with explicit benefits

- Upgrade options for specific services (priority boarding, seat selection)

What doesn't work:

- Hidden fees that feel like punishment

- Confusing tier requirements

- Benefits that don't match the price premium

The lesson? Service tiers work when they feel like upgrades, not extortion.

Why Service Tiers Work for Everyone

For Customers: Choice and Transparency

You get what you pay for. No more wondering why your service experience sucks when you bought the cheapest option. No more paying premium prices for economy service.

You can choose your experience. Need basic service for a simple purchase? Save money. Want VIP treatment for something important? Pay for it.

Expectations align with reality. No more promise/delivery gaps because you know exactly what level of service you purchased.

For Companies: Aligned Incentives

Service becomes a profit center. Instead of minimizing service costs, companies can maximize service value. Better service drives more revenue.

Customer lifetime value clarity. Premium service customers pay premium prices. Companies know exactly how much they can invest in keeping these customers happy.

Differentiation through service. When products become commoditized, service becomes the differentiator. Companies can compete on service quality, not just price.

Predictable service costs. Instead of absorbing unpredictable service demands, companies can budget for specific service levels.

For Service Workers: Career Growth

Service quality matters. When companies make money from service, they reward employees who deliver great service.

Clear career progression. Junior reps handle Tier 1, senior reps handle Tier 3+, specialists handle Concierge. Skills development has direction.

Better tools and training. When service generates revenue, companies invest in the people and systems that deliver it.

Implementation: How Companies Can Make the Transition

Phase 1: Audit Current Service Costs

Most companies have no idea what they actually spend on customer service per customer. Companies can't price service tiers without understanding current costs.

Calculate the real cost of service:

- Fully loaded cost per customer service interaction

- Average interactions per customer per year

- Cost differences between channel types (phone vs. email vs. chat)

- Hidden costs (escalations, refunds, management time)

Segment customers by service usage:

- Low-touch customers (rarely contact service)

- Standard customers (occasional service needs)

- High-touch customers (frequent service users)

- Problem customers (disproportionate service demands)

Phase 2: Design Tier Structure

Start with three tiers: Basic (included), Standard (+25%), Premium (+50%). Don't try to do everything at once.

Define clear benefits for each tier:

- Response time guarantees

- Channel access (email only vs. phone vs. dedicated rep)

- Hours of availability

- Escalation procedures

- Special perks (extended returns, priority shipping, etc.)

Price based on value, not cost: What would customers pay for guaranteed 2-hour response time? For a dedicated rep who knows their account? Price to value, then work backward to cost structure.

Phase 3: Test with New Customers

Don't force existing customers into tiers immediately. Start by offering service tier choices to new customers. Let existing customers opt in when they're ready.

A/B test the messaging:

- "Service levels" vs. "Support packages" vs. "Care plans"

- Emphasis on choice vs. emphasis on quality

- Annual pricing vs. per-incident pricing

Measure everything:

- Uptake rates for each tier

- Customer satisfaction by tier

- Cost per customer by tier

- Revenue impact

Phase 4: Expand and Optimize

Add advanced tiers based on demand: If 20% of customers choose Premium, there's probably demand for Ultra-Premium.

Customize by industry: B2B customers might value dedicated account managers. B2C customers might prefer extended hours and fast response times.

Build service quality into pricing: Tie tier pricing to measurable service quality metrics. Guarantee specific outcomes.

Industry-Specific Applications

Banking

- **Basic:** Online banking, standard fees, email support

- **Standard:** Phone support, reduced fees, priority processing

- **Premium:** Personal banker, waived fees, 24/7 support

- **Private:** Dedicated wealth manager, exclusive services, concierge banking

Healthcare

- **Basic:** Standard appointments, regular wait times, automated reminders

- **Standard:** Shorter wait times, nurse hotline, online portal

- **Premium:** Same-day appointments, 24/7 telemedicine, care coordination

- **Concierge:** House calls, executive physicals, unlimited access

Telecommunications

- **Basic:** Standard service, automated support, basic speed

- **Standard:** Priority repair, human support, enhanced speed

- **Premium:** 24/7 support, guaranteed uptime, business-grade service

- **Enterprise:** Dedicated account team, custom solutions, guaranteed SLAs

Retail

- **Basic:** Self-service returns, email support, standard shipping

- **Standard:** Phone support, easy returns, expedited shipping

- **Premium:** Personal shopping, white-glove delivery, styling services

- **VIP:** Personal stylist, exclusive access, home delivery with setup

Common Objections (And Why They're Wrong)

"Customers will revolt if we charge for service"

Wrong. Customers revolt when they pay premium prices for terrible service. They're fine paying for good service if the value is clear.

Evidence: Apple Care, Amazon Prime, airline first class, hotel elite status programs. Customers pay for service upgrades constantly when they know what they're getting.

"This will create a two-tier system where poor people get bad service"

Wrong. This creates a transparent system where service quality matches price paid. The current system creates a hidden lottery where everyone randomly gets terrible service regardless of what they paid.

Better: A world where someone can choose basic service for basic prices, and upgrade when they need better service.

"Our competitors will undercut us if we charge for service"

Right. And they'll provide worse service because they're not being paid to provide good service. Let them race to the bottom. Companies that choose service tiers are racing to the top.

Long-term: Customers will pay more for better service. The competitor offering "free" terrible service will lose customers to companies with clear service options over time.

"This is too complicated for customers to understand"

Wrong. Customers understand airline fare classes, hotel room categories, and restaurant pricing tiers. They can understand service tiers.

Key: Make the tiers and benefits crystal clear. Don't hide the value proposition in fine print.

The Psychology of Choice

Here's something fascinating: Customers are happier with tiered service even when they choose the lowest tier.

Why? Because choice creates ownership. When you choose Basic Service and get basic service, you're satisfied because you got what you chose. When you pay an unknown amount for unknown service and get bad service, you feel ripped off.

Choice reduces complaints. When customers select their service level, they have realistic expectations.

Choice increases loyalty. Customers who actively choose to pay for premium service become more invested in the relationship.

Choice reveals true preferences. Companies learn what customers actually value, not what they say they value in surveys.

The Competitive Cascade

Service tiers create a competitive cascade that benefits everyone:

Early Adopters gain first-mover advantages by offering transparent choice while competitors hide service costs.

Fast Followers adapt quickly to avoid competitive disadvantage as customers learn to expect service choice.

Late Adopters are forced to offer service tiers to remain competitive, but lose the differentiation advantages.

Holdouts become increasingly disadvantaged as service transparency becomes customer expectation.

The companies that move first capture the customers who are willing to pay for better service. The companies that move last get the customers who aren't.

The Network Effect

Service tiers create network effects that accelerate adoption:

Customer Education: Each company that offers service tiers educates customers about the value of explicit service choice.

Worker Mobility: Service workers who experience tier-based systems demand similar clarity in their next jobs.

Investor Interest: Successful service tier implementations attract investor attention and capital.

Media Coverage: Service tier success stories get shared, creating positive examples for other companies.

Regulatory Momentum: Service tier transparency can inform regulatory approaches to consumer protection.

The Future of Service

In five years, I predict service tiers will be as common as airline fare classes. Companies that cling to the "service is free" lie will lose customers to companies that offer honest choices.

The companies that win will:

- Offer clear, valuable service tier options

- Deliver on their service promises consistently

- Use service quality as a competitive differentiator

- Treat service as a profit center, not a cost center

The companies that lose will:

- Continue hiding service costs in product prices

- Promise great service while cutting service budgets

- Treat all customers the same regardless of what they pay

- Wonder why their customer satisfaction scores keep declining

Your Role in the Service Tier Revolution

As a customer, you can accelerate this transition:

Ask companies about service tiers. "Do you offer different levels of customer support?" Even if they don't, you're planting a seed.

Pay for good service when it's offered. Vote with your wallet for companies that give you service choices.

Leave reviews that mention service quality. Help other customers understand what level of service to expect.

Demand transparency in service pricing. Ask customer service reps how much of your purchase price goes toward support.

As a business leader, you can lead this change:

Calculate your real service costs. You can't price what you can't measure.

Test service tiers with a subset of customers. Start small, learn fast, scale what works.

Train your team to sell service value. Service isn't a cost, it's a product with real benefits.

Measure service Return on Investment. Track how service quality affects customer lifetime value and referral rates.

The Bottom Line

We've spent decades pretending customer service is free. It's not. It never was. And pretending it has created a system where everyone loses.

Customers lose because they pay hidden service fees for terrible service.

Companies lose because they can't invest appropriately in service quality.

Service workers lose because they're treated like costs instead of value creators.

The service tier revolution fixes all of this. It brings honesty to service pricing. It aligns incentives between customers and companies. It rewards service excellence instead of service avoidance.

The question isn't whether service tiers will become standard. The question is whether your company will lead the change or follow it.

Because somewhere, right now, a customer is gladly paying $6,000 a year for great customer service.

And they're telling all their friends about it.

The revolution in honest service pricing has begun. The only question is will YOU be part of it.

Next: Now that we understand how to make good service economically viable through honest pricing, let's explore how to use technology to deliver that service better than ever before without replacing the human connection that customers actually value.

CHAPTER 8

TECHNOLOGY THAT SERVES HUMANS

How to build automation that helps instead of hides

I'm sitting in the call center of a major insurance company in Dallas, watching something beautiful happen.

A customer calls in furious. His claim was denied. He's been transferred three times. He's ready to scream.

The rep's name is Maria. She pulls up his account. But instead of seeing a basic customer record, she sees something remarkable:

The AI Assistant's Assessment:

- "Customer likely frustrated due to 3 previous transfers"

- "Claim denial appears to be processing error - original photos show clear damage"

- "Customer has been loyal for 12 years, never filed fraudulent claim"

- "Recommended action: Approve claim immediately, apologize for delays"

- "Suggested follow-up: Call customer in 3 days to ensure satisfaction"

Maria doesn't read from a script. She doesn't put the customer on hold to "research" his issue. She says:

"Mr. Johnson, I can see exactly what happened here, and I'm sorry. This claim should have been approved immediately. I'm processing that now, and you'll see the payment in your account tomorrow morning. I'm also crediting your account for the inconvenience, and I'll personally call you Friday to make sure everything was handled properly."

Call time: 3 minutes. Customer satisfaction: Through the roof. Maria's stress level: Minimal.

This is what happens when technology makes humans superhuman instead of making humans obsolete.

The Current Tech Tragedy

Most customer service technology is designed with one goal: avoid talking to customers. It's built on the assumption that human interaction is expensive and should be minimized.

This creates systems that:

- Hide information from customers instead of providing it

- Frustrate customers into giving up instead of helping them succeed

- Make service reps less effective instead of more capable

- Create barriers between problems and solutions instead of removing them

The result? Technology that nobody likes. Customers hate it. Service reps hate it. Even the executives who bought it secretly hate it; they just can't admit it because they spent millions on it.

But there's a different way. Technology that serves humans instead of replacing them.

The Human-First Tech Philosophy

Before companies build any customer service technology, they should ask one question: "Does this make the human interaction better or worse?"

If the answer is "worse" or "there is no human interaction," they're building the wrong thing.

Human-first technology follows three principles:

1. Augment, Don't Replace

Technology should make service reps smarter, faster, and more empowered not obsolete.

Bad tech: Chatbot that tries to handle complex billing disputes

Good tech: AI that instantly pulls up customer history, previous complaints, payment patterns, and suggests resolution options

2. Reduce Friction, Don't Create It

Every piece of technology should eliminate steps between customers and solutions.

Bad tech: Phone tree with 47 options that eventually leads to "please visit our website"

 Good tech: System that recognizes your phone number, predicts why you're calling, and routes you to the right expert immediately

3. Enable Choice, Don't Force Compliance

Give customers multiple ways to interact and let them choose what works for them.

Bad tech: "All customer service is now handled through our app"

 Good tech: "Contact us by phone, email, chat, text, or app whatever works best for you"

The Human-First Tech Stack

Here's what customer service technology looks like when it's designed to serve humans:

Layer 1: Context Intelligence

What it does: Gives service reps complete customer context before the interaction starts.

Instead of this conversation:

- "Can I get your account number?"

- "Can you verify your address?"

- "What's the nature of your call today?"

- "Let me transfer you to billing..."

You get this:

"Hi Sarah, I can see you're calling about the charge on your account from last Tuesday. I've already pulled up the transaction details and I can help you with that right now."

How it works:

- Customer calls from registered phone number

- System instantly displays: purchase history, recent interactions, account status, payment history, known preferences

- AI analyzes recent account activity and predicts likely reason for call

- System routes to rep with expertise in that area

- Rep sees suggested talking points and resolution options

The technology:

- CRM integration with real-time data sync

- Machine learning models trained on call patterns

- Intelligent call routing based on customer profile and issue type

- Mobile-optimized rep interface with voice-to-text for note-taking

Layer 2: Decision Support Intelligence

What it does: Gives reps AI-powered suggestions for resolving issues quickly and appropriately.

Instead of this:

- Rep: "Let me check with my supervisor..."

- Customer: waits 8 minutes

- Rep: "I can offer you a $10 credit."

- Customer: "That doesn't solve anything."

You get this:

Rep: "I can see this is your third call about this issue, and you've been a customer for 5 years. I have several options I can offer you right now..."

AI suggests three resolution paths with predicted customer satisfaction scores

How it works:

- AI analyzes similar cases and their outcomes

- System suggests resolution options ranked by customer satisfaction probability

- Rep can see the customer impact of each option (financial, emotional, time)

- System provides scripting suggestions for difficult conversations

- Real-time coaching prompts for emotional situations

The technology:

- Natural language processing for understanding customer sentiment

- Machine learning models trained on successful resolutions

- Integration with company policy database and approval workflows

- Real-time coaching engine with escalation triggers

Layer 3: Proactive Prevention Intelligence

What it does: Identifies and prevents problems before customers experience them.

Instead of this:

Customer discovers problem → gets frustrated → calls to complain → service rep apologizes and fixes it

You get this:

System detects potential problem → automatically fixes what it can → proactively notifies customer about what it couldn't fix → offers compensation for inconvenience

How it works:

- System monitors for service disruptions, shipping delays, billing errors, etc.

- AI predicts which customers will be most impacted

- Automated systems fix simple issues (refunds, credits, rebookings)

- Human reps handle complex cases with full context and pre-approved solutions

- Proactive communication keeps customers informed

The technology:

- IoT sensors and system monitoring for real-time issue detection

- Predictive analytics for identifying at-risk customers

- Automated workflow engines for standard resolutions

- Multi-channel communication systems for proactive outreach

Layer 4: Learning and Improvement Intelligence

What it does: Continuously learns from every interaction to improve the entire system.

Instead of this:

Same problems happen repeatedly → customers complain about the same issues → no one connects the dots

You get this:

System identifies patterns in customer issues → suggests product improvements → recommends policy changes → trains AI models on successful interactions

How it works:

- Every customer interaction is analyzed for themes and sentiment

- System identifies root causes of frequent complaints

- AI suggests process improvements and policy changes

- Machine learning models continuously improve based on outcome data

- Feedback loops to product and operations teams

The technology:

- Advanced analytics and pattern recognition

- Sentiment analysis and theme extraction

- A/B testing frameworks for process improvements

- Integration with product development and operations teams

Real-World Implementation: Case Studies

Case Study 1: The Credit Card Company That Eliminated Hold Time

The Problem: Average hold time of 12 minutes, customer satisfaction score of 32%, high rep turnover.

The Human-First Solution:

- **Context Intelligence:** System recognizes customer phone number and pulls up recent transactions, payment history, and previous service interactions

- **Predictive Routing:** AI predicts reason for call based on recent account activity and routes to specialist immediately

- **Decision Support:** Reps get real-time suggestions for credit limits, fee reversals, and retention offers based on customer profile

- **Proactive Prevention:** System automatically detects and fixes billing errors before customers notice them

Results:

- Average hold time: 0 minutes (direct to specialist)

- First-call resolution: 87% (up from 34%)

- Customer satisfaction: 78% (up from 32%)

- Rep satisfaction: 91% (up from 23%)

What changed: Reps went from being information gatherers to problem solvers. Technology handled the busywork so humans could focus on empathy and complex reasoning.

Case Study 2: The E-commerce Company That Made Returns Effortless

The Problem: Returns process took 45 minutes on average, required multiple emails, frustrated customers and reps.

The Human-First Solution:

- **Smart Return Detection:** AI analyzes return request and automatically approves 80% based on customer history and product type

- **Context-Aware Processing:** For complex returns, reps see full order history, photos, return reason patterns, and suggested resolutions

- **Proactive Communication:** System automatically updates customers on return status and proactively offers solutions (exchanges, credits, replacements)

- **Learning Loop:** Every return interaction teaches the system to better predict customer needs and streamline the process

Results:

- Return processing time: 3 minutes average (down from 45)

- Customer effort score: 8.7/10 (up from 3.2/10)

- Return-related complaints: Down 89%

- Rep productivity: Up 340%

What changed: Returns went from adversarial negotiations to collaborative problem-solving. Technology eliminated the bureaucracy so humans could focus on finding the right solution.

Case Study 3: The Healthcare Company That Made Insurance Navigable

The Problem: Patients couldn't understand their benefits, claims were confusing, prior authorization took weeks.

The Human-First Solution:

- **Benefits Translation:** AI converts insurance jargon into plain English explanations tailored to each patient's situation

- **Predictive Authorization:** System predicts which procedures will need prior auth and starts the process automatically

- **Personalized Guidance:** Reps get patient-specific talking points and can see exactly what the patient's plan covers for their situation

- **Proactive Outreach:** System identifies patients likely to have billing questions and reaches out with explanations before they call confused

Results:

- Call volume: Down 60% (proactive education)

- Prior authorization time: 2 days average (down from 14)

- Patient understanding: Up 400% (measured by follow-up questions)

- Clinical staff satisfaction: Up 78% (less time on administrative tasks)

What changed: Healthcare became collaborative instead of adversarial. Technology translated complexity into clarity so humans could focus on care.

Implementation Guide: Building Human-First Technology

Step 1: Audit Your Current Tech Stack

Questions to ask:

- Does this technology help reps solve problems faster?

- Does it give customers more choices or fewer choices?

- Does it reduce the number of steps between problem and solution?

- Do customers prefer using it or avoiding it?

- Do reps say it makes their job easier or harder?

Red flags:

- Technology that increases call volume instead of decreasing it

- Systems that require extensive training for basic tasks

- Tools that customers actively try to bypass

- Technology that makes reps less knowledgeable about customer needs

Step 2: Start with Context, Not Automation

Most companies try to automate interactions before improving them. Start by giving humans better information.

Phase 1 priorities:

- **Single customer view:** One screen with everything about this customer

- **Interaction history:** What happened in previous contacts with this customer

- **Predictive insights:** Why is this customer likely calling today?

- **Resolution suggestions:** What has worked for similar situations?

Step 3: Automate the Busywork, Not the Relationship

Identify tasks that add no value to the customer relationship and automate those first.

Good automation targets:

- Data entry and note-taking

- Account lookups and verification

- Simple transaction processing

- Appointment scheduling

- Status updates and notifications

Bad automation targets:

- Complex problem diagnosis

- Emotional or sensitive conversations

- Policy exception decisions

- Complaint resolution

- Relationship building

Step 4: Build Learning Loops

Every customer interaction should make the system smarter.

Data to capture:

- Which resolution approaches work best for different customer types

- What information reps need most frequently

- Which policies cause the most confusion

- What proactive communications prevent problems

How to use it:

- Continuously improve AI suggestions

- Update rep training based on successful interactions

- Recommend policy changes based on customer feedback patterns

- Optimize workflows based on rep behavior

Step 5: Measure Human Outcomes, Not Just System Metrics

Traditional metrics:

- Average handle time

- Cost per contact

- Automation rate

- Deflection rate

Human-first metrics:

- First-call resolution rate

- Customer effort score

- Rep empowerment rate (how often reps can solve problems without escalation)

- Customer emotional outcome (frustrated to satisfied)

- Rep job satisfaction and retention

The Technology Companies Need to Stop Building

Chatbots That Pretend to Be Human

The problem: They create uncanny valley experiences that frustrate customers and damage trust.

The alternative: Chatbots that are obviously bots but incredibly useful. "I'm a bot, but I can instantly process your return, refund your account, or connect you to the right human for complex issues."

IVR Systems That Hide Humans

The problem: Phone trees designed to prevent customer to rep interaction instead of optimizing it.

The alternative: Smart routing that uses customer data to predict needs and connect to the right specialist immediately.

AI That Replaces Human Judgment

The problem: Automated decision-making for complex situations that require empathy and context.

The alternative: AI that provides information and suggestions to humans who make the final decisions.

Self-Service That Forces Compliance

The problem: Eliminating human alternatives to force customers into automated systems.

The alternative: Self-service that's so good customers choose it, with human backup always available.

Advanced Implementation: The Complete Framework

The Technology Selection Matrix

Before investing in any customer service technology, score it on these dimensions:

Customer Impact (1-10):

- Does it solve customer problems faster?

- Does it reduce customer effort?

- Does it improve emotional outcomes?

Rep Empowerment (1-10):

- Does it give reps better information?

- Does it increase their problem-solving capability?

- Does it reduce their stress and frustration?

Business Value (1-10):

- Does it improve key metrics (satisfaction, retention, referrals)?

- Does it reduce operational costs sustainably?

- Does it create competitive differentiation?

Implementation Feasibility (1-10):

- Can it integrate with existing systems?

- Do you have the skills to implement it well?

- Will your team actually use it?

Minimum viable score: 32/40. If a technology scores below 32, don't buy it.

The Integration Roadmap

Month 1-2: Foundation

- Audit current technology and customer pain points

- Map customer journey and identify friction points

- Assess rep tools and capabilities

- Define success metrics

Month 3-4: Quick Wins

- Implement basic context intelligence

- Improve routing based on customer data

- Add simple decision support tools

- Train reps on new capabilities

Month 5-8: Scale and Optimize

- Deploy advanced AI assistance

- Build proactive monitoring systems

- Create learning loops and feedback mechanisms

- Expand to all customer touchpoints

Month 9-12: Innovation and Leadership

- Develop predictive prevention capabilities

- Build industry-leading customer experience

- Share success stories and best practices

- Plan next phase of evolution

Technology Vendor Evaluation Framework

When selecting vendors, use this checklist:

Technical Capability: ☐ Real-time data integration

☐ Machine learning that improves over time

☐ Mobile-first design for reps

☐ Open APIs for customization

☐ Scalable architecture

Human-Centricity: ☐ Enhances rather than replaces human capability

☐ Reduces customer effort

☐ Improves rep job satisfaction

☐ Provides easy human escalation

☐ Respects customer choice

Business Value: ☐ Measurable Return on Investment within 12 months

☐ Competitive differentiation potential

☐ Sustainable cost structure

☐ Risk mitigation capabilities

☐ Growth enablement

Implementation Support: ☐ Proven track record with similar

companies

☐ Comprehensive training and change management

☐ Ongoing optimization and improvement

☐ Strong customer success organization

☐ Clear escalation and support processes

The Future of Human-First Technology

In five years, I predict the best customer service will be invisible. Not because it's automated, but because it's so good it prevents problems instead of just solving them.

What this looks like:

- Your bank calls you before fraudulent charges appear on your statement

- Your airline rebooks you on a better flight before your original flight gets delayed

- Your insurance automatically approves claims before you even know you need to file them

- Your software fixes bugs in your specific configuration before you experience them

The technology that enables this:

- IoT sensors that detect problems in real-time

- Predictive analytics that identify issues before they impact customers

- Automated resolution systems for standard problems

- Human experts for complex situations with full context and authority

The human role evolves:

- From reactive problem-solving to proactive relationship management

- From script-following to creative problem-solving

- From cost center to profit center

- From damage control to customer advocacy

Red Lines: When NOT to Automate

Here's when to skip the bots and go straight to humans:

- Billing errors

- Cancellations

- Complaints

- Medical issues

- Fraud reports

- Grieving customers

- Anything that starts with: "I've already tried the app..."

- "I am choosing to speak to a human"

These are not "routine." These are moments that matter. Handle them like they do.

Your Technology Buying Guide

Before you invest in any customer service technology, use this checklist:

☐ Does it make customer problems easier to solve?

☐ Does it give reps better tools to help customers?

☐ Does it reduce the number of steps between problem and solution?

☐ Does it provide customers with more choices, not fewer?

☐ Does it learn from every interaction to improve the next one?

☐ Can it integrate with your existing systems?

☐ Do your reps actually want to use it?

☐ Would you want to interact with this technology as a customer?

If you can't answer yes to at least 7 of these 8 questions, don't buy it.

The Bottom Line on Technology

Technology isn't the enemy of good customer service. Bad technology is.

The difference is simple: Good technology serves humans. Bad technology replaces them.

When companies build technology that makes humans superhuman instead of making humans obsolete, something magical happens:

- Customers get better service
- Reps have better jobs
- Companies make more money
- Everyone wins

The question isn't whether to use technology in customer service. The question is whether to use it to help humans or hide from them.

Choose wisely. Your customers and your conscience are watching.

The dream of automation was never to dehumanize service. It was to make the human parts better.

That only happens when we stop chasing buzzwords and start asking the only question that matters:

Does this make the customer feel more seen? Or less?

If it's more: build it.
 If it's less: scrap it.

Technology is a tool. Not a shield. Not a substitute. Not a scapegoat.

The future isn't bots vs. people.
 It's bots with people.

And when we get that right, customer service stops being something we endure and becomes something we actually appreciate.

CHAPTER 9

THE CUSTOMER REVOLT HANDBOOK

Tactical guide for consumers who want to fight back

The hold music stops. A human voice says, "Thank you for calling. I see you've been a customer for eight years. I've already pulled up your account and I can see exactly why you're calling. Let me fix that for you right now."

Three minutes later, your problem is solved. You hang up feeling... confused. Because that never happens.

But it did happen. To me. Last week. And it reminded me of something important: good customer service still exists. We've just stopped demanding it.

We've been conditioned to accept garbage. To expect nothing. To feel grateful when someone barely does their job.

That ends now.

This isn't about being a Karen. This isn't about screaming at minimum-wage workers who didn't create the policies that torture you. This is about strategic customer advocacy. About using your power as a revenue source to demand the treatment you've already paid for.

Because here's the truth: You have more power than you realize. You just don't know how to use it.

The Pre-Purchase Audit: Don't Give Your Money to Enemies

Before you buy anything more expensive than lunch, screen the company like you're hiring them. Because you are.

The Customer Service Test Drive

Step 1: Call Before You Buy

Find their customer service number. If it takes more than 30 seconds to locate on their website, that's a red flag. If there's no number at all, run.

Call it. Time the experience:

- How many menu options before you reach a human?

- How long is the hold?

- Does the rep sound like they want to help or want to die?

If you can't reach a helpful human in under 5 minutes for a simple question, imagine what happens when you have a real problem.

Step 2: The Return Policy Reality Check

Every company has a return policy. Most of them are lies.

Try this: Ask the rep, "If I needed to return this, what exactly would I need to do?" Listen for:

- Vague language ("Just contact us")

- Hidden fees ("Restocking charges may apply")

- Impossible timelines ("Must be returned in original packaging within 48 hours")

- Runaround ("You'd need to speak to a different department")

If they can't explain the return process clearly, the return won't be clear either.

Step 3: The Social Media Stress Test

Go to their Twitter or Facebook page. Ignore the marketing posts. Look at the replies.

Scroll through customer complaints. How do they respond?

- Do they respond at all?

- Are the responses helpful or corporate-speak?

- Do they solve problems publicly or just say "DM us"?

- How recent are the complaints? (If people stopped complaining, they probably stopped buying)

Step 4: The Reddit Reality Check

Search Reddit for the company name plus "customer service" or "support." Reddit users don't lie about service experiences. They're brutal, honest, and detailed.

Look for patterns:

- The same complaints appearing repeatedly

- Stories about being transferred endlessly

- People warning others not to buy from this company

If the Reddit consensus is "avoid at all costs," believe them.

The Service Quality Checklist

Before you hand over your credit card, the company should earn a "yes" on at least 8 of these 10 questions:

☐ Can I reach a human in under 3 minutes?

☐ Can I find their phone number without a treasure hunt?

☐ Do they have multiple ways to contact them? (phone, email, chat)

☐ Is their return policy written in plain English?

☐ Do they respond to social media complaints professionally?

☐ Are their hours reasonable for my time zone?

☐ Can the first person I talk to actually help me, or do they just transfer?

☐ Do they have generally positive reviews for service (not just product)?

☐ Can I cancel/return/modify without talking to "retention specialists"?

☐ Do they proactively communicate about delays, outages, or problems?

Score below 8? Find a competitor. Your future self will thank you.

The Escalation Playbook: How to Get Results When Things Go Wrong

When customer service fails you, most people give up or explode. Both are mistakes. Here's how to escalate strategically.

Level 1: The Professional Persistence Method

Document Everything

Before you even make the first call, create a simple record:

- Date and time of each interaction

- Name of every person you speak with

- Summary of what they promised

- Reference numbers, case numbers, ticket numbers

This isn't paranoia. This is evidence.

The Opening Script That Works

"Hi, I'm calling about [specific issue]. This is my [second/third/fourth] time calling about this. I spoke with [name] on [date] who told me [specific thing]. That didn't resolve it, so I need to escalate this. Can you help me, or should I ask for a supervisor right now?"

This tells them:

- You're organized
- You're persistent
- You remember details
- You're not going away

The Follow-Up Method

After every call, send an email summarizing what was discussed and what was promised. Use the rep's name if you have it.

"Hi [Name], thanks for your help today. Just to confirm, you said you would [specific action] by [specific date]. My reference number is [X]. I'll follow up if I don't hear back by then."

This creates a paper trail and accountability.

Level 2: The Strategic Supervisor Request

When to Escalate

- The rep says "I can't do that" without explaining why
- You've been transferred more than twice
- They're reading from a script and can't deviate
- They make promises but don't follow through
- The solution doesn't match the problem

How to Ask

Don't say: "Let me speak to your manager!"

Do say: "You have been great! This issue is beyond what you are empowered to help with. I need to speak with someone who has more authority to solve this. Can you transfer me to a supervisor or manager?"

The Supervisor Conversation

"Hi, I need your help. I've been trying to resolve [issue] for [timeframe]. I've spoken with [names] and tried [solutions]. None of that worked. I need someone with the authority to [specific outcome]. Can you help me or direct me to someone who can?"

Level 3: The Executive Email Campaign

When front-line service fails, go to the top. Not to scream, but to inform.

Finding Executive Emails

Most follow patterns:

- firstname.lastname@company.com

- flastname@company.com

- first.last@company.com

Try the CEO, CFO, and Chief Customer Officer. Use LinkedIn to verify names.

The Executive Email Template

Subject: Customer Service Failure - Account [Your Account Number]

[Executive Name],

I'm writing because your customer service system has failed to resolve a simple issue, and I think you'd want to know about it.

SUMMARY:

- I've been a customer for [timeframe]

- Issue: [brief description]

- Attempted resolution: [what you tried]

- Current status: [still unresolved]

- Business impact: [how this affects you]

EVIDENCE:

[attach timeline of interactions]

[include representative names and promises made]

[reference numbers/case numbers]

RESOLUTION REQUEST: [specific, reasonable outcome you want]

I'm not looking to blame anyone, but this experience doesn't match the service standards your company advertises. I'd appreciate your help resolving this quickly.

[Your name]

[Your contact information]

[Your account information]

Why This Works

- It's professional, not emotional
- It includes specific details
- It suggests you understand this isn't normal
- It asks for help, not revenge

Level 4: The Public Pressure Campaign

When private escalation fails, make it public. But do it strategically.

Social Media Escalation

Don't just vent. Create pressure.

The Twitter Template

"Hey @CompanyName, I've been trying to resolve [issue] for [timeframe]. Spoke with [names], tried [solutions]. Still waiting for [outcome]. Case #[number]. Can you help? #CustomerService"

Why This Works

- It's factual, not emotional
- It includes specifics they can look up
- It's public but not abusive
- It shows you've tried proper channels

The Review Strategy

Write detailed, factual reviews on:

- Google Reviews
- Yelp
- Better Business Bureau
- Industry-specific sites (TripAdvisor for travel, etc.)

The Review Template

"I've been a customer since [date]. Overall, [product/service] has been [honest assessment]. However, their customer service needs improvement.

Issue: [specific problem]

Resolution attempts: [what you tried]

Outcome: [current status]

Time invested: [hours/days]

This experience was frustrating because [specific reason]. I'd recommend this company if they improve their service responsiveness."

Update Your Review

If they fix your problem, update your review to reflect that. Companies notice when negative reviews turn positive.

Level 5: The Regulatory Option

For serious issues, regulatory agencies have power that customer service departments don't.

When to Use This

- Financial services: billing disputes, unauthorized charges

- Telecommunications: service outages, billing errors

- Healthcare: insurance denials, privacy violations

- Travel: flight delays, refund denials

- Auto: warranty disputes, recall issues

Key Agencies

- Consumer Financial Protection Bureau (CFPB) - financial companies

- Federal Communications Commission (FCC) - telecom/internet

- Department of Transportation (DOT) - airlines

- State Attorney General - local businesses

- Better Business Bureau - general complaints

Filing an Effective Complaint

- Use specific facts, not emotions

- Include timeline and documentation

- Explain financial impact

- State what resolution you want

- Follow up on the complaint status

The Coalition Strategy: When Individual Action Isn't Enough

Sometimes your problem isn't unique. Sometimes the company is systematically screwing an entire group of customers.

Finding Your Tribe

Reddit Communities

Subreddits like r/[CompanyName] often become informal support groups for frustrated customers. Share your experience and see if others have the same issue.

Facebook Groups

Search for "[Company Name] customers" or "[Industry] complaints." These groups often organize collective action.

Class Action Lawsuits

For widespread issues (especially financial harm), lawyers organize class actions. Websites like ClassAction.org track active cases.

Organizing Collective Pressure

The Coordinated Review Bomb

If dozens of customers have the same issue, coordinate posting reviews on the same day. This creates a spike that the company's reputation management team will notice.

The Social Media Storm

Agree on a specific day and hashtag. Everyone posts their story at the same time. This can trend and create media attention.

The Executive Email Flood

Multiple customers emailing executives about the same issue on the same day signals a systemic problem, not isolated complaints.

Advanced Tactics: When You're Fighting Monopolies

Some companies think they're too big to care. Phone companies, internet providers, utilities often have captive customers and act like it.

The Regulatory Complaint Strategy

These companies fear regulators more than individual customers.

For Internet/Phone Service

File FCC complaints at consumercomplaints.fcc.gov. Companies are required to respond within 30 days. I've seen internet outages fixed within hours of FCC complaints being filed.

For Utilities

Contact your state public utilities commission. These agencies have power over rates and service quality.

For Airlines

File DOT complaints at www.transportation.gov. Airlines hate DOT attention because it can lead to fines.

The Political Pressure Play

Contact Your Representatives

Local politicians want to help constituents with concrete problems. A phone call from a senator's office carries weight.

The Template Email to Representatives

Subject: Constituent Service Issue - [Company Name]

Dear [Representative Name],

I'm a constituent in [district/city] experiencing ongoing issues with [company name]. This appears to be a widespread problem affecting many of your constituents.

Issue: [brief description]

Attempted resolution: [what you tried]

Business impact: [how it affects you and others]

I'm writing because this company appears to be taking advantage of their market position to provide poor service while maintaining high prices. This affects many residents in our area.

Could your office help facilitate a resolution or investigate whether this is a broader consumer protection issue?

[Your name and address]

The Media Attention Strategy

Local News Loves David vs. Goliath Stories

Local TV stations and newspapers need content. A well-documented customer service horror story, especially if it affects multiple people, can become a news story.

The Media Pitch Template

Subject: Story Tip - Local Residents Struggling with [Company] Service

Hi [Reporter Name],

I have a story tip that might interest your viewers. [Company] appears to be systematically providing poor service to customers in [area], despite [relevant context - high prices, monopoly position, etc.].

I've documented my experience over [timeframe] and found [number] other customers with similar issues.

The story includes:

- [specific examples]

- [financial impact]

- [company's inadequate responses]

- [broader implications for consumers]

I have documentation and can connect you with other affected customers.
Would this be of interest for a consumer protection segment?

[Your contact information]

The Nuclear Option: Strategic Departure

Sometimes the best customer service strategy is becoming someone else's customer.

The Cancellation Conversation

Don't just cancel. Use your departure as leverage.

The Script That Gets Attention

"I'm calling to cancel my service. Before you transfer me to retention, let me explain why: [specific service failures]. I've tried to resolve this [number] times over [timeframe]. I'm not looking for discounts or promotions. I need to know if you can guarantee these service issues will be fixed. If not, please cancel my account."

Why This Works

- You're not asking for free stuff

- You're offering them a chance to fix the real problem

- You're making it clear that money isn't the issue

- You're speaking their language (customer retention metrics)

The Exit Interview Email

After you leave, send feedback to executive leadership explaining exactly why you left and what it would take to win you back.

Many companies have win-back campaigns for departed customers. Your feedback might influence policy changes that help future customers.

Your Daily Customer Service Habits

Screenshot Everything

Save confirmation emails, chat transcripts, order numbers. Your phone's screenshot folder should look like evidence for a court case.

Use Credit Cards, Not Debit

Credit cards have better dispute processes and fraud protection. Your bank will fight harder for their money than yours.

Read the Fine Print on Returns

Before you buy, know exactly how to return it. Screenshot the return policy in case they change it later.

Keep Receipts in Email

Email yourself pictures of receipts immediately. Paper fades, but email is forever.

Document Promised Delivery Dates

Screenshot the estimated delivery date when you order. If they change it later, you have proof of what was promised.

The Long Game: Building a Service-Focused Economy

Every time you choose a company with better service over one with lower prices, you're voting for the economy you want.

Reward Good Service Loudly

Leave glowing reviews for companies that treat you well. Tag them on social media with positive stories. Refer friends to businesses that earn it.

Punish Bad Service Quietly

Don't give abusive companies the attention of angry rants. Just stop buying from them and tell others to do the same.

Pay for Service When It's Worth It

If a company charges more but provides dramatically better service, pay it. You're investing in a business model you want to see more of.

Share Your Tactics

When these strategies work for you, teach them to others. The more customers who know how to effectively advocate for themselves, the more companies will have to adapt.

Your 30-Day Challenge

Pick one company that has consistently disappointed you but that you keep using out of habit or convenience.

This month, find an alternative. Research their service reputation. Test their customer support. Switch if they're better.

If you can't find a better alternative, use the escalation strategies in this chapter to demand better service from your current provider.

Document the experience. See what works. Refine your approach.

Then do it again next month with a different company.

Because here's what I've learned after decades in this industry: Companies change when customers demand change. Not before.

You have the power. You've always had the power.

You just needed to know how to use it.

The Customer Service Bill of Rights

As we build this movement, here's what we're fighting for:

1. The Right to Reach a Human Within 3 Minutes

Any company offering support must provide direct human access within 180 seconds.

2. The Right to Cancel Easily

You should be able to cancel using the same method you used to sign up.

3. The Right to Transparent Support Metrics

Companies must publish monthly statistics: hold times, resolution rates, satisfaction scores.

4. The Right to Escalate Without Obstruction

Clear, working path to supervisors and specialists without IVR loops or chatbot dead ends.

5. The Right to Be Heard by Humans

No AI-only resolution for billing errors, legal issues, or contract disputes.

The Revolution Begins With You

We don't fix service by begging. We fix it by punishing bad behavior and rewarding good behavior.

You are not just a customer. You are the revenue. Act like it.

Every purchasing decision is a vote. Every complaint is leverage. Every switch to a competitor is a signal.

Companies will provide the level of service that customers demand and reward. No better. No worse.

The revolution in customer service doesn't start with corporate boardrooms or government regulations.

It starts with you. Refusing to accept terrible treatment. Demanding the service you've already paid for. Using your power as a revenue source to force change.

The companies that treat you well will get your money and your advocacy. The companies that treat you badly will get neither.

It's time to stop being victims of customer service and start being its revolutionaries.

The revolt begins now.

CHAPTER 10

THE SERVICE PROFESSIONAL'S REVOLUTION

For those inside the system who want to fix it

L et's start with a blunt truth: If your CEO isn't bought in for the long term, you need to change their mind or change your CEO.

That's not hyperbole. If your CEO sees service as a short-term nuisance instead of a long-term asset, your progress is capped. No matter how visionary you are, no matter how clever your tactics, you will hit a ceiling.

You know the system is broken. You've lived it.

You've watched executives nod thoughtfully at customer satisfaction scores while slashing headcount. You've seen brilliant reps quit because they were tired of being measured on call duration instead of problem resolution. You've built chatbots that frustrate customers and demoralize the humans who have to clean up their mess.

But here's what most people don't understand: you want to fix it more than anyone.

The customers only feel the pain when they call. You live with it every day.

So this chapter isn't about convincing you that change is needed. This is your tactical guide for making it happen even when your CEO sees service as a cost center and your CFO treats human empathy like a line item to be optimized away.

For those of you with leadership backing or the power to create it this is your playbook.

The Service Leader's Dilemma

Let me tell you about Christine. She's a VP of Customer Experience at a mid-size SaaS company. Smart, experienced, genuinely cares about customers. Last quarter, she presented a plan to reduce customer churn by 15% through better service.

The plan would cost $2.8 million annually. It would save $4.1 million in retained revenue.

Her CEO said no.

Why? Because the cost hits this year's budget, but the revenue impact takes 18 months to show up. And this CEO's bonus is tied to this year's margins.

Sound familiar?

This is why good service leaders burn out. You're playing chess while everyone else is playing checkers. You're thinking in customer lifetime value while they're thinking about quarterly earnings calls.

But here's the thing Christine learned and what I want to teach you: You don't need to change their minds. You need to change their incentives.

The Business Case That Actually Works

Forget satisfaction scores. Forget NPS. Forget "customer delight." None of that moves executives who see service as a necessary evil.

Here's what does:

The Revenue Protection Model

Frame service as insurance, not investment. Your job isn't to create happy customers, it's to prevent revenue hemorrhaging.

The Math That Matters:

- Customer acquisition cost vs. retention cost (retention is always cheaper)
- Lifetime value of customers who receive good vs. poor service
- Viral coefficient of satisfied vs. dissatisfied customers (word of mouth amplification)
- Cost of crisis management when service failures go public

The Presentation That Wins:

Don't ask for a service investment. Ask for churn prevention funding.

"We're losing $X per month to preventable cancellations. This program plugs that leak and costs less than replacing those customers."

The Competitive Advantage Play

If your industry has universally terrible service (and most do), good service becomes a differentiator that marketing can't buy.

The Research:

- How much does your company spend on customer acquisition?
- What's your close rate on sales calls?
- How many prospects mention service concerns during the sales process?

The Pitch:

"While our competitors are cutting service costs, we're going to win market share by being the company people actually want to call."

The Crisis Prevention Insurance

Every company has service fires. The question is whether you're fighting them or preventing them.

The Historical Analysis:

- Track every service crisis from the past 2 years
- Calculate the real cost: executive time, PR damage, customer credits, lost deals
- Show how better frontline service could have prevented 80% of them

The Value Prop:

"This isn't about being nice to customers. This is about not having to explain to the board why we're trending on Twitter for all the wrong reasons."

Implementation Roadmap: From Broken to Revolutionary

Phase 1: Stop the Bleeding (First 90 Days)

Week 1-2: Audit the Pain

Don't start with solutions. Start with evidence.

- Record 50 real customer calls (get their permission)
- Document every policy that makes reps say "I'm sorry, but I can't..."
- Track the true cost of escalations: time, resources, senior leader involvement
- Survey your reps anonymously: "What policy would you change if you could?"

Week 3-4: Pick Your Battle

Choose ONE thing that causes the most customer and employee pain. Not everything. One thing.

Examples:

- The policy that requires supervisor approval for refunds under $50

- The system that makes customers repeat their information three times

- The script that prohibits reps from saying "I don't know, but I'll find out"

Week 5-8: Run the Pilot

Change that one thing for a small group of reps. Measure everything:

- Customer satisfaction for those interactions

- Rep stress levels and job satisfaction

- Time to resolution

- Number of escalations

- Revenue impact (credits given, customers retained)

Week 9-12: Build the Case

Document the results obsessively. Create before/after stories. Get quotes from customers. Film testimonials from reps. Make the success undeniable.

Phase 2: Scale What Works (Months 4-12)

Expand the Pilot

Roll your successful change to more reps, more customers, more situations. But resist the urge to fix everything at once. Build momentum with wins.

Train for Empowerment

Most service training teaches scripts and procedures. Revolutionary service training teaches judgment and advocacy.

New Training Focus:

- "How to be a customer detective" (understanding the real problem)
- "The escalation conversation" (when and how to involve supervisors)
- "The recovery framework" (turning problems into loyalty)
- "Policy translation" (explaining company rules in human language)

Hire for Humans

Stop hiring for "customer service experience." Start hiring for emotional intelligence, problem-solving ability, and genuine empathy. These people exist. You just haven't been looking for them.

Interview Questions That Matter:

- "Tell me about a time you bent a rule to do the right thing."
- "How would you explain a frustrating policy to an angry customer?"

- "What's the difference between being helpful and being nice?"

Phase 3: Systemic Change (Year 2-3)

Redesign Metrics

Stop measuring what's easy to count. Start measuring what actually matters.

Metrics That Drive Good Behavior:

- First-call resolution rate (did we solve it without transfers?)
- Customer effort score (how hard was it to get help?)
- Rep empowerment rate (how often do reps solve problems without escalation?)
- Relationship NPS (would you want to talk to this specific rep again?)

Technology That Serves Humans

Most service tech is designed to replace humans. Revolutionary service tech is designed to make humans superhuman.

Tech Stack Priorities:

- Context systems: One screen that shows everything about this customer
- Decision support: AI that suggests solutions, not scripts

- Escalation intelligence: Systems that route complex issues to the right expert immediately
- Follow-up automation: Technology that ensures promises get kept

Culture Change

The hardest part isn't changing policies. It's changing the cultural assumption that customers are interruptions instead of opportunities.

Cultural Shifts to Drive:

- From "deflection" to "resolution"
- From "contain costs" to "create value"
- From "follow the script" to "solve the problem"
- From "manage the call" to "serve the human"

Overcoming Internal Resistance

The CFO Who Hates Customer Service

Their concern: "Service is a cost center. Every dollar we spend there is a dollar we can't spend on growth."

Your response: Show them the leaky bucket. Calculate customer lifetime value. Prove that retention is cheaper than acquisition. Frame service as revenue protection, not expense.

The magic phrase: "We're not asking to spend more on service. We're asking to stop losing money on preventable churn."

The Sales Leader Who Blames Service

Their concern: "We bring in the customers, service drives them away."

Your response: Make service a sales enabler. Show how good service creates referrals, increases expansion revenue, and shortens sales cycles when prospects aren't worried about getting stuck with terrible support.

The magic phrase: "What if prospects asked to talk to our customers because they'd heard our service was so good?"

The Marketing Leader Who Doesn't Want Truth

Their concern: "If we promise great service, we have to deliver great service."

Your response: Help them understand that authentic service stories are more powerful than manufactured brand messages. Real customer advocacy beats paid advertising.

The magic phrase: "What if our customers did our marketing for us?"

The CEO Who Wants Quick Wins

Their concern: "This sounds expensive and slow."

Your response: Start with one high-impact, low-cost change that creates visible results fast. Then reinvest the success into bigger changes.

The magic phrase: "Let's prove this works with the smallest possible investment, then scale what succeeds."

The Secret Weapon: Your Frontline

Your customer service reps are sitting on a goldmine of intelligence that the rest of your company desperately needs.

They know:

- Which products break most often
- Which policies cause the most confusion
- Which competitors customers are considering
- Which features customers actually want
- Which marketing messages don't match reality

Create a feedback loop that matters:

- Weekly "rep intelligence" reports to product teams

- Monthly policy review sessions with actual reps

- Quarterly "voice of customer" presentations to executives

- Annual "rep recommendations" that get implemented

Make your frontline feel like consultants, not cattle. When they see their insights driving real change, they'll become your biggest advocates for customer-centric transformation.

The Economics of Service Excellence

Return on Investment Calculation Framework

Here's how to calculate the real return on service investment:

Revenue Protection:

- Current churn rate × Average customer value = Monthly revenue at risk

- Service improvement impact on churn × Monthly revenue at risk = Monthly revenue protected

- Annual revenue protected ÷ Annual service investment = Revenue protection Return on Investment

Customer Lifetime Value Enhancement:

- Average CLV for customers with good service experience
- Average CLV for customers with poor service experience
- Difference × Number of customers affected = Total CLV impact

Word-of-Mouth Multiplier:

- Net Promoter Score improvement
- Referral rate increase
- Cost per acquisition savings from referrals
- Brand reputation impact on conversion rates

Crisis Prevention Savings:

- Historical cost of service-related crises
- Frequency reduction from better frontline service
- Executive time savings
- Legal and PR cost avoidance

The Service Investment Portfolio

Treat service improvements like an investment portfolio with different risk/return profiles:

Quick Wins (3-6 months):

- Policy changes that eliminate obvious pain points
- Basic empowerment that reduces escalations
- Simple technology fixes that improve rep efficiency
- Expected Return on Investment: 200-500%

Medium-term Investments (6-18 months):

- Comprehensive training programs
- Technology upgrades that enhance human capability
- Hiring improvements and retention programs
- Expected Return on Investment: 150-300%

Long-term Transformations (18+ months):

- Cultural change initiatives
- Industry-leading service standards
- Competitive differentiation through service excellence

- Expected Return on Investment: 300-1000%

Advanced Strategies for Service Leaders

The Trojan Horse Method

When direct advocacy for service investment fails, embed service improvements in other initiatives:

- **Digital Transformation Projects:** Include human-centered design requirements
- **Cost Reduction Initiatives:** Show how service excellence reduces total cost of ownership
- **Customer Experience Programs:** Position service as the delivery mechanism for CX promises
- **Employee Engagement Efforts:** Demonstrate how service empowerment improves retention

The Pilot-and-Scale Strategy

Start small, prove value, scale success:

1. Identify the highest-impact, lowest-risk improvement
2. Run controlled pilot with measurable success metrics

3. Document results with customer and employee stories

4. Present expansion as risk mitigation, not new investment

5. Scale systematically while measuring compounding returns

The Competitive Intelligence Approach

Use competitor service failures to justify your service investments:

- Monitor competitor service failures on social media

- Document their crisis management costs

- Show how your service excellence captures their dissatisfied customers

- Position service leadership as competitive moat

The Customer Advisory Board Leverage

- Create formal customer input into service strategy:

- Establish quarterly customer advisory sessions

- Include service quality as standing agenda item

- Document customer willingness to pay for service excellence

- Use customer voices to advocate internally for service investment

Beyond Traditional Metrics

Traditional Service Metrics:

- Average handle time (incentivizes rushing)
- Cost per contact (incentivizes deflection)
- First call resolution (incentivizes false closure)
- Customer satisfaction (easily gamed)

Revolutionary Service Metrics:

- Customer effort score (how hard was it to get help?)
- Emotional outcome tracking (frustrated → satisfied journey)
- Rep empowerment index (how often can reps solve problems without escalation?)
- Relationship quality score (would the customer want the same rep next time?)
- Service-driven revenue (sales and retention attributed to service quality)

The Service Dashboard That Matters

Customer Health Indicators:

- Percentage of customers who've had positive service experience
- Trend in service-related churn
- Customer lifetime value by service experience quality
- Net Promoter Score segmented by service interaction history

Employee Engagement Indicators:

- Rep job satisfaction and retention
- Percentage of reps who feel empowered to help customers
- Internal referral rate for service positions
- Career advancement within service organization

Business Impact Indicators:

- Service-attributed revenue growth
- Crisis prevention savings
- Word-of-mouth marketing value
- Competitive wins attributed to service reputation

Building Your Service Revolution Coalition

Internal Allies

Finance Partners: Show them the revenue protection math and crisis prevention savings

HR Partners: Demonstrate how service excellence improves employee retention and satisfaction

Product Partners: Share customer insights that drive product improvements

Marketing Partners: Provide authentic customer stories and advocacy content

Sales Partners: Prove how service quality affects deal closure and expansion

Executive Sponsorship

CEO Engagement:

- Frame service as brand protection and competitive advantage
- Provide monthly customer story updates (both positive and negative)

- Include service metrics in board presentations
- Connect service quality to strategic initiatives

Board Education:

- Include customer service quality in board materials
- Bring customer voices into board meetings
- Show correlation between service investment and business outcomes
- Position service excellence as risk mitigation strategy

External Validation

Industry Recognition:

- Apply for customer service awards and certifications
- Speak at industry conferences about service innovation
- Publish case studies about service transformation success
- Participate in customer service research and benchmarking

Customer Advocacy:

- Feature customer testimonials about service quality
- Create customer reference programs highlighting service
- Encourage customers to share service stories publicly
- Use customer advisory feedback to justify service investments

The Technology Integration Strategy

Human-First Technology Implementation

Phase 1: Context and Information

- Implement unified customer view for all reps
- Add intelligent routing based on customer history
- Provide real-time coaching and suggestion tools
- Create seamless escalation pathways

Phase 2: Prediction and Prevention

- Deploy predictive analytics for customer issues
- Implement proactive outreach for at-risk accounts
- Add automated resolution for routine problems

- Create feedback loops for continuous improvement

Phase 3: Intelligence and Optimization

- Use AI to identify patterns in customer issues

- Implement dynamic policy recommendations

- Create personalized service experiences

- Build learning systems that improve over time

Technology Vendor Selection

Key Evaluation Criteria:

✓ Enhances rather than replaces human capability

✓ Provides measurable customer experience improvements

✓ Integrates seamlessly with existing systems

✓ Scales with business growth

✓ Includes comprehensive training and support

✓ Offers clear Return on Investment measurement tools

✓ Aligns with human-centered service philosophy

Crisis as Opportunity

When service failures create change windows, here's how to leverage these moments:

Immediate Response (First 48 hours):

- o Document the failure's root causes systematically
- o Calculate the total cost including hidden impacts
- o Identify what better service could have prevented
- o Prepare preliminary improvement recommendations

Analysis Phase (First 2 weeks):

- o Conduct thorough post-mortem with all stakeholders
- o Survey affected customers about their experience
- o Analyze similar failures at competitor companies
- o Develop comprehensive prevention strategy

Investment Proposal (Week 3-4):

- o Present service investment as crisis prevention insurance

- o Show Return on Investment calculation based on avoided future crises
- o Include customer feedback supporting the need for change
- o Request expedited approval based on urgency

Implementation Planning (Month 2):

- o Begin immediate fixes while planning systemic changes
- o Communicate changes to customers and employees
- o Set measurable goals for improvement
- o Create regular reporting on progress

Your 90-Day Action Plan

Month 1: Foundation Building

Week 1: Complete current state audit and pain point analysis

Week 2: Identify highest-impact improvement opportunity

Week 3: Build coalition of internal allies and gather supporting data

Week 4: Develop pilot program proposal with clear success metrics

Month 2: Pilot Execution

Week 5-6: Launch pilot program with selected team and customers

Week 7-8: Monitor results, gather feedback, refine approach

Month 3: Scaling Preparation

Week 9-10: Document pilot results and create scaling plan

Week 11-12: Present results to leadership and request scaling approval

Ongoing: Culture and System Change

Monthly service quality reviews with leadership

Quarterly customer advisory sessions

Annual service strategy planning

Continuous measurement and improvement

What Victory Looks Like

You'll know you've succeeded when:

Customers say:

"I actually don't mind calling them."

"They fixed it faster than I expected."

"The person I talked to seemed like they cared."

Reps say:

"I can actually help people here."

"Management listens to our ideas."

"I'm proud to tell people where I work."

Executives say:

"Service is a competitive advantage."

"Our customers are our best marketing."

"I want to add more service people, not fewer."

The market says:

Customers choose you because of service reputation

Competitors try to copy your service approach

Industry analysts cite you as service leadership example

Recruitment becomes easier as word spreads about your service culture

Career Development in Service Excellence

Service Professional Track:

Frontline representative → Senior specialist → Team lead → Manager →
Director → VP

Focus on customer outcome expertise and team development

Compensation tied to customer success metrics and team performance

Service Innovation Track:

Analyst → Specialist → Program manager → Strategy director → Chief
Customer Officer

Focus on service design, technology integration, and business strategy

Career advancement based on innovation impact and business results

Cross-Functional Leadership:

Service excellence experience as requirement for general management

Service leadership as pathway to CEO and board positions

Service expertise valued in consulting and advisory roles

Industry Transformation

Your success becomes part of industry-wide transformation:

Competitive Pressure: Your service excellence forces competitors to improve or lose market share

Talent Migration: Employees trained in your service culture spread practices to other companies

Best Practice Sharing: Your innovations become industry standards and benchmarks

Customer Expectations: Your service quality raises customer expectations across the industry

This Is Bigger Than You Think

This isn't just a corporate initiative. It's not a CX refresh. This is a social movement.

There isn't a political movement in the world with this much agreement. Left, right, young, old we are united in our hatred of customer service.

And it's not just customers. People who work in customer service hate it, too.

The frontline is burned out. The customers are worn down. Technology is alienating. The incentives are misaligned.

But the good news? That much unity is a tremendous source of power.

We can take it down. We can build something better. Something human. Something worthy.

Call to Arms

This is not a small transformation. It's a redefinition of what service means. Of what loyalty means. Of how businesses grow in the age of infinite choice and automated indifference.

The revolution in customer service starts with professionals like you who refuse to accept that terrible service is inevitable. Who understands that the technology and knowledge exist to create something better. Who is willing to do the work to build it.

Your customers are waiting. Your reps are hoping. Your company needs it.

The choice is yours: Keep managing the broken system, or start building the one that actually works.

The revolution begins with you.

And when you succeed, your customers won't just thank you. They'll stay, spend, and bring others with them.

That's not just good service. That's good business.

The question isn't whether you can fix customer service. The question is whether you will.

The tools are here. The roadmap is clear. The movement is growing.

What are you waiting for?

CHAPTER 11

WHAT VICTORY LOOKS LIKE

We've spent most of this book diagnosing what's wrong with customer service and explaining why it stays broken. We've provided tactical solutions for customers, service professionals, and business leaders who want to create change.

But after 55,000 words of problems and solutions, you might be wondering: what does victory actually look like? What happens when customer service works the way it should?

This isn't fantasy. This isn't utopian thinking. This is what customer service looks like right now at companies that have chosen to compete on service excellence rather than service avoidance.

Let me show you what becomes possible when companies honor the promises they make to customers.

A Day in the Life: When Service Works

It's Tuesday morning. Your smart coffee maker stops working the one you bought six months ago that's been perfect until today. Instead of dreading the customer service call, you actually feel confident about getting help.

You open the company's app. Before you even navigate to support, a notification pops up: "We've detected an issue with your coffee maker. Tap here for instant help."

You tap. A chat window opens: "Hi Sarah, I can see your Model X-200 hasn't connected to WiFi since 6:47 AM. Our sensors show this is likely the heating element issue we discovered in units manufactured January 15-30. Yours was made on January 22."

"Can it be fixed?" you type.

"Unfortunately, no. But I can send you a replacement today with same-day delivery. You'll have it by 2 PM. I'll also include a prepaid return label for the defective unit. And since this was our manufacturing error, I'm crediting your account $25 for the inconvenience."

"That's... really generous," you type.

"Not really. You trusted us with your money and we gave you a defective product. The least we can do is make it right quickly and acknowledge that we wasted your time."

Total interaction time: 90 seconds. Problem solved. No phone trees, no hold music, no asking if you tried unplugging it. Just a system that detected the problem and a human-AI partnership that resolved it instantly.

At 1:47 PM, your new coffee maker arrives. It works perfectly. The next morning, you get a text: "How's your new coffee maker working? Reply STOP to opt out, or let us know if you need anything else."

Two weeks later, you're recommending the company to a friend who needs a coffee maker. Not because the product is perfect, but because you trust that if something goes wrong, they'll fix it.

The hardest part of this book was gathering examples of companies who have done great work in this space. All of these are flawed but it gives hope for what is possible.

Case Study 1: Chewy-When E-commerce Has a Heart

In 2011, Ryan Cohen and Michael Day launched Chewy with a simple premise: what if an online retailer actually cared about customers as much as Amazon cared about logistics?

They picked the pet supply market, a $95 billion industry dominated by big-box retailers and Amazon. On paper, they had no chance. Amazon had better prices, faster shipping, and infinite inventory.

What Chewy had was something Amazon couldn't replicate: genuine emotional connection with customers.

The Chewy Difference

Pet-Centric Support: Customer service reps aren't trained in order fulfillment they're trained in pet care. When you call about dog food, they ask about your dog's age, breed, activity level, and health issues. They make recommendations based on your pet's needs, not profit margins.

Emotional Intelligence at Scale: When a customer's pet dies, Chewy sends handwritten condolence cards not automated emails, actual handwritten notes from customer service reps. When pets are sick, they've been known to send flowers. When customers can't afford emergency vet bills, they've provided free food and supplies.

Unconditional Returns: If your pet doesn't like the food, return it even if the bag is empty. If you ordered the wrong size collar, they'll send the right one and tell you to donate the wrong one to a local shelter rather than returning it.

Proactive Pet Care: Their autoship program doesn't just deliver food on schedule it includes reminders for vet checkups, notifications about food recalls, and access to veterinary consultations.

The Business Results

This wasn't charity, it was strategy. And it worked:

$10.7 billion revenue in 2023: More than Petco and PetSmart combined

95%+ customer retention rate: Compared to Amazon's 75% in pet categories

2x higher lifetime value: Average Chewy customer spends $1,400 annually vs $700 for typical e-commerce pet spending

Profitable growth: Consistently profitable while Amazon's pet category loses money trying to compete on price

What This Proves

Chewy proved that even in the age of Amazon, customers will choose higher prices for better service. They showed that emotional connection scales. Most importantly, they demonstrated that service excellence isn't just good for customers it's good for business.

Ryan Cohen sold Chewy to PetSmart for $3.35 billion in 2017. The acquisition was based almost entirely on Chewy's customer relationships and service culture.

Case Study 2: Chick-fil-A - Service Excellence at Scale

Fast food is supposed to be a commodity business. Cheap food, fast service, minimal human interaction. McDonald's perfected this model decades ago.

Chick-fil-A decided to compete differently. Instead of faster and cheaper, they chose better and more human.

The Service Model

"My Pleasure" Culture: Employees say "my pleasure" instead of "you're welcome." It sounds trivial, but it creates a different emotional tone in every interaction. Customers notice the difference.

Face-to-Face Ordering: While competitors deploy kiosks and apps to eliminate human contact, Chick-fil-A employees take drive-through orders using tablets while talking to customers face-to-face. Technology serves human connection rather than replacing it.

Immediate Problem Resolution: Any employee can provide free meals, refunds, or extras to resolve issues immediately. No manager approval required for customer satisfaction decisions under $20.

Wait Time Management: If drive-through wait exceeds 3 minutes, free items are automatically offered. Not because of policy, but because they understand that time is valuable and delays should be acknowledged.

The Economics of Excellence

The results speak for themselves:

$18.8 billion revenue (2023): Despite being closed Sundays

$8.7 million revenue per restaurant: vs industry average of $1.2 million

Highest customer satisfaction in fast food: 20+ points above nearest competitor (McDonald's)

Limited expansion: Growth constrained by ability to maintain service standards, not market demand

The Scalability Question

Chick-fil-A proves that service excellence scales. They operate over 3,000 locations with consistent service quality. The key isn't technology or policies, it's culture and training.

New employees spend 40+ hours in training before serving customers. Franchisees are selected based on alignment with service values, not just financial capability. Regional managers spend most of their time on service quality, not cost optimization.

The investment in service training pays for itself through higher revenue per location and lower employee turnover (60% below industry average).

Case Study 3: Shopify - B2B Service as Competitive Advantage

When Tobias Lütke launched Shopify in 2006, he was competing against established e-commerce platforms like Magento and WooCommerce. His technical background was in programming, not customer service.

But Lütke understood something crucial: in B2B software, customer success isn't a nice-to-have; it's the difference between growth and churn.

The Support Philosophy

Response Time as Product Feature: Average 2.3 minutes to reach a human via chat or phone. This isn't marketed as "fast support" , it's built into the product experience as a core feature.

Technical Expertise: Support reps aren't just order-takers reading scripts. They're trained in web development, payment processing, international commerce, and business strategy. When merchants call, they get actual expertise.

Solution Authority: Reps can provide technical solutions, account credits, and policy exceptions without escalation. They're empowered to solve problems, not just document them.

Proactive Merchant Success: Before major platform changes, Shopify contacts affected merchants personally to explain impacts and provide migration assistance. They measure success by merchant success, not internal efficiency metrics.

The Business Impact

Shopify's service-first approach created competitive advantages that traditional metrics don't capture:

4.6+ million merchants globally: Growing 20%+ annually despite increased competition

97% customer retention rate: In an industry where 60-70% is considered good

Support satisfaction scores of 4.8/5: Consistently across all channels and languages

> **Word-of-mouth growth:** 35% of new merchants cite existing merchant recommendations as primary decision factor

The B2B Lesson

Shopify proves that in B2B, service quality directly affects customer lifetime value. When merchants succeed, Shopify succeeds. When merchants struggle with technical issues, they stop growing, which limits Shopify's revenue growth.

This alignment of incentives creates genuine partnership rather than vendor-customer relationships. Shopify's support team isn't a cost center, they're growth enablers.

> ## Case Study 4: Apple's Service Transformation (2020-2024)
>
> For years, Apple customer service was a paradox. Beautiful products, terrible support experience. Long wait times, confusing policies, repair processes that felt deliberately obstructive.
>
> Then something changed. Between 2020-2024, Apple systematically transformed their service experience while maintaining their premium positioning.

What Changed?

Genius Bar Evolution: Eliminated appointments for many   common issues. Added walk-up support for basic problems. Created express lanes for simple repairs and quick questions.

Seamless Channel Integration: Chat, phone, and in-store support share complete customer context. You can start a conversation via chat, continue it over phone, and finish it in-store without repeating information.

Repair Transparency: Real-time repair status updates via text and email. Parts availability alerts before you schedule appointments. Clear cost estimates before any work begins.

Problem Ownership: For complex issues spanning multiple products, Apple assigns single points of contact who coordinate across different support teams.

The Measurement

Apple's service transformation is measurable:

- Customer satisfaction improved from 76 (2019) to 87 (2024): Based on post-interaction surveys

- **Support call volume decreased 30%:** While customer base grew 25%, indicating better first-contact resolution

- **AppleCare attachment rates increased:** As trust in support improved, more customers opted for extended service plans

- **Repair satisfaction scores up 40%:** Previously the biggest source of customer complaints

The Strategic Shift

Apple's transformation wasn't about cost reduction, it was about competitive positioning. As hardware becomes commoditized, service becomes a differentiator.

The investment in service training, technology, and staffing was significant. But it positioned Apple for long-term customer relationships rather than just product transactions.

Most importantly, it proved that large companies can change service culture when leadership commits to the transformation.

Case Study 5: Warby Parker - Service as Market Disruption

In 2008, four Wharton students were frustrated by overpriced eyewear and poor service from established optical chains. They decided to build a company that competed primarily on service rather than product innovation.

The eyewear market was dominated by Luxottica (LensCrafters, Pearle Vision, Sunglass Hut) and characterized by high prices, limited selection, and sales-focused interactions.

The Service Innovation

Home Try-On: Five frames shipped free. Try them at home for five days. Return what you don't want, buy what you love. Eliminated the pressure and uncertainty of in-store selection.

Virtual Try-On with Human Support: AR technology to see frames on your face, combined with live style consultations with human experts. Technology enhanced human advice rather than replacing it.

> **Prescription Guarantee:** Free replacement for prescription errors, damage, or customer dissatisfaction within 30 days. Risk-free trial period for something as personal as eyewear.

> **Seamless Omnichannel:** Online and retail store experiences seamlessly connected. Shared customer data, unified inventory, consistent service standards.

Market Impact

Warby Parker's service-first approach forced industry transformation:

- **$3+ billion valuation:** Based primarily on customer relationships and service differentiation
- **85% customer retention rate:** In industry where 40-50% was typical
- **3+ pairs per customer:** vs industry average of 1 pair every 2-3 years

- **Competitive Response:** Established players forced to improve service, offer home try-on programs, and reduce pressure sales tactics

The Disruption Model

Warby Parker proved that established industries can be disrupted through service excellence rather than just technology innovation. They didn't invent better glasses, they invented better customer experience.

The model has been replicated across industries: Casper (mattresses), Dollar Shave Club (razors), Glossier (cosmetics). In each case, service excellence disrupted established players who competed primarily on distribution and marketing.

The Service Tier Revolution in Action

Beyond individual company excellence, we're seeing systematic adoption of transparent service pricing, the service tier model discussed in Chapter 7.

Tesla's Service Evolution

Tesla's service tier options represent the future of honest service pricing:

Tesla Service Tiers

Basic Service: Scheduled maintenance at service centers, mobile service for simple issues, online support. Included with vehicle purchase.

Premium Service: Priority scheduling, loaner vehicles, direct technical specialist access. $2,400 annually.

Concierge Service: Vehicle pickup/return with detailing, 24/7 support, personal service advisor. $6,000 annually.

Results: Net Promoter Score of 87 for Concierge customers vs 31 for Basic Service customers. Premium customers report higher overall satisfaction with their vehicle ownership experience.

Amazon Prime's Tier Evolution

Amazon Prime started as shipping benefits but evolved into comprehensive service tiers:

Amazon Service Tier

Prime: Faster shipping, basic customer service, some entertainment content.

Prime Business: Dedicated account management, bulk pricing, advanced analytics.

Prime Enterprise: Custom pricing, white-glove onboarding, guaranteed SLAs.

Each tier provides explicitly different service levels, and customers choose based on their needs rather than being forced into one-size-fits-all service.

The Economics of Service Excellence

When companies provide excellent customer service, they don't just create happy customers they create economic advantages that compound over time:

Lower Customer Acquisition Costs

Word-of-mouth referrals from satisfied customers cost 5x less than paid advertising and convert at 3x higher rates. Chewy gets 40% of new customers through referrals. Shopify's referral rate drives 35% of merchant growth.

Higher Customer Lifetime Value

Customers who trust a company's service stick around longer and spend more money over time. Chick-fil-A customers visit 3x more frequently than McDonald's customers. Apple customers replace devices less frequently but buy more accessories and services.

Premium Pricing Power

Companies known for excellent service can charge higher prices because customers value the service insurance they're buying. Warby Parker glasses cost more than online competitors but less than traditional optical chains positioning in the value sweet spot.

Reduced Service Costs

Companies that solve problems right the first time spend less on repeat contacts, escalations, and complaint management. Apple's first-contact resolution improvements reduced total service costs by 18% while improving satisfaction.

Employee Retention

Workers want to be part of organizations that treat customers well. Chick-fil-A's employee turnover is 60% below industry average. Shopify's customer success team has 95% annual retention vs industry average of 68%.

Brand Resilience

Companies with strong service reputations recover faster from product problems, bad publicity, or competitive challenges. Apple maintained customer loyalty through multiple product controversies because service excellence created relationship resilience.

The Ripple Effects: How Good Service Changes Everything

When customer service works properly, the benefits extend far beyond individual transactions:

Trust in Institutions

People who experience competent, respectful service from companies are more likely to trust other institutions, government, healthcare, education. Good service experiences create optimism about institutional competence.

Economic Productivity

Time not spent fighting with customer service is time available for productive work, family relationships, and community engagement. McKinsey estimates that poor customer service costs the U.S. economy $75 billion annually in lost productivity.

Innovation Incentives

Companies competing on service quality invest in innovations that actually help customers rather than innovations that help companies avoid customers. Service-driven R&D creates products people want rather than products companies can sell cheaply.

Worker Dignity

Employees who can actually help customers experience job satisfaction and professional pride rather than burnout and cynicism. Service excellence creates positive employment experiences that extend beyond individual companies.

Social Cohesion

Positive daily interactions with institutions that serve our needs create optimism about cooperation and shared problem-solving. Good service experiences contribute to social trust and civic engagement.

What the Future Looks Like

Imagine an economy where customer service excellence is the norm rather than the exception:

Competition: Companies compete primarily on service quality rather than just price and features. Marketing focuses on service promises that companies actually keep rather than aspirational messaging.

Technology: AI and automation enhance human capability rather than replacing human connection. Technology makes service more personal and effective, not less personal and more frustrating.

Employment: Customer service becomes a respected profession with career advancement opportunities, professional development, and compensation that reflects the value created.

Culture: Society expects and rewards institutions that serve human needs effectively. Customer-centric thinking influences how we design everything from government services to healthcare systems.

This isn't utopian fantasy. Every element exists somewhere today. The question is whether we can scale these examples and make them normal rather than exceptional.

The Network Effect of Change

Customer service excellence creates network effects that accelerate adoption:

Customer Expectations: Every positive service experience raises customer expectations for all other companies. Chewy's pet owners expect better service from their vet clinics. Chick-fil-A customers expect more courtesy from other retailers.

Employee Movement: Workers who experience good service cultures demand similar cultures in their next jobs. They carry service excellence practices to new companies and industries.

Investor Interest: Companies that demonstrate service-driven growth attract investors who understand that customer relationships are valuable assets. Service excellence becomes an investment thesis.

Media Attention: Service excellence stories get shared more widely than service failure stories, creating positive examples that other companies want to emulate.

Each company that chooses service excellence makes it easier for others to follow.

The Transformation Timeline

Large-scale change in customer service excellence follows a predictable pattern:

Phase 1: Early Adopters (2020-2027)
Companies like Chewy, Shopify, and Chick-fil-A prove that service excellence is profitable. Early majority companies begin experimenting with service differentiation.

Phase 2: Competitive Pressure (2027-2032)

Service quality becomes a mainstream competitive factor as customers increasingly choose based on service reputation. Late majority companies adopt service improvements to avoid competitive disadvantage.

Phase 3: Industry Standards (2032-2037)

Service excellence becomes table stakes rather than differentiation as industry norms shift toward customer-centric practices. Regulatory standards codify minimum service requirements.

Phase 4: Cultural Norm (2037+)

Customer service excellence becomes so normal that companies providing poor service are seen as obviously dysfunctional rather than acceptably cost-optimized.

We're currently in early Phase 1, with isolated examples of excellence and growing awareness that the current system is unsustainable.

Your Role in Creating Victory

The transformation to service excellence doesn't happen automatically. It requires conscious choices by customers, service professionals, business leaders, and policymakers:

As a Customer: Reward companies that provide excellent service with loyalty, referrals, and premium pricing. Punish companies that provide terrible service by switching providers and sharing your experiences.

As a Service Professional: Advocate for service excellence within your organization. Measure success by customer outcomes rather than internal efficiency. Build the business case for service investment using the examples in this chapter.

As a Business Leader: Treat customer service as a competitive advantage rather than a cost center. Study the companies in this chapter and adapt their strategies to your industry. Invest in service excellence as a long-term growth strategy.

As a Citizen: Support regulations that protect customers from systematic service abuse. Demand that government services meet the same standards you expect from private companies.

The Promise of Victory

Victory in customer service doesn't mean perfection. It means competence, respect, and accountability as normal rather than exceptional.

It means technology that helps rather than hides. Companies that keep their promises. Workers who can actually help. Systems designed for human dignity rather than corporate extraction.

It means calling customer service without dread, knowing that you'll reach someone who can and will help you solve your problem quickly and respectfully.

This isn't too much to ask. It's what we've already paid for. It's what we deserve. And increasingly, it's what we can demand and receive.

The examples in this chapter prove that excellent customer service is possible, profitable, and sustainable. The question isn't whether it can be done, it's whether we have the will to do it.

Your Next Steps

If you're a customer frustrated with terrible service: Visit WaitingForService.com and download the Customer Advocacy Toolkit. Join thousands of others who are learning to demand better treatment and actually get it.

If you're a service professional wanting to drive change: Sign up for the Service Leader Newsletter at WaitingForService.com. Get monthly insights, implementation guides, and connections with other professionals building service excellence.

If you're a business leader ready to compete on service: Contact me directly through WaitingForService.com to discuss speaking engagements, strategic consulting, or executive advisory services. Let's build your competitive advantage through service excellence.

If you're a media professional covering customer service issues: Reach out through WaitingForService.com for expert commentary, data analysis, and insider perspective on industry trends and policy implications.

If you're anyone who believes customer service can be better: Share this book. Post your own service experiences. Support companies that treat customers well. Punish companies that don't.

Every action matters. Every choice counts. Every person who refuses to accept terrible service makes it easier for the next person to demand better.

The Promise

This movement will succeed because it serves everyone's interests:

Customers get the treatment they've already paid for.

Service professionals get jobs worth having.

Business leaders get sustainable competitive advantages.

Society gets institutions that work for people instead of against them.

The tools exist. The knowledge exists. The examples exist.

What's been missing is the will to change and the community to support that change.

Now you have both.

EPILOGUE: THE PLAN AHEAD

There are many theories about why customer service is so poor. Most of them miss the mark.

Some blame technology. Others blame outsourcing. Some point to corporate greed. Others blame customer expectations or generational differences or global competition.

These explanations treat customer service failure as an accident, a series of unfortunate decisions that somehow led us astray from better times.

But that's not what happened.

This Went According to Plan

My entire career has been spent in customer service. I have worn all the hats—consultant, executive, system builder, crisis manager. I've been inside the budget meetings where customer service gets defunded. I've watched executives nod at customer satisfaction scores while cutting headcount. I've built some of the technology that frustrates you today.

What we've learned is that customer service has gone according to plan. The economic incentives around customer service are largely to blame for every grievance we have against it.

This isn't broken. This is the business model.

Every minute you spend on hold, every transfer between departments, every chatbot that can't understand your question, every policy that seems designed to frustrate you—these aren't accidents. They're spreadsheet decisions made by rational people optimizing for rational goals.

The problem isn't that companies don't know how to provide good customer service. The problem is that they've discovered they can profit more by providing bad customer service.

Why This Book Mattered Now

We've been living through the largest crisis of trust between companies and customers in modern history.

Customer service has become so universally terrible that we've stopped expecting it to work. We've learned to solve problems ourselves, work around broken systems, and accept frustration as the price of modern commerce.

But this acceptance has created massive economic and social costs that most people don't see:

Economic costs: Bad customer service destroys enormous amounts of value through lost productivity, failed businesses, and misallocated resources. When millions of people spend hours every day fighting with customer service systems, that's millions of hours not spent on productive work.

Social costs: Customer service interactions are often the primary relationship between citizens and the economy that serves them. When those interactions are systematically dehumanizing, they erode trust in institutions, markets, and the social contract itself.

Innovation costs: Companies that compete on cost-cutting rather than customer satisfaction create a race to the bottom that discourages innovation, investment in quality, and long-term thinking.

Human costs: The front-line workers who absorb customer rage while being powerless to solve systemic problems are burning out, quitting, and losing faith in work itself.

The customer service crisis isn't just about inconvenience. It's about whether we can build an economy that serves human needs or whether we'll accept an economy that systematically frustrates them.

What We've Discovered

This book has taken you on a journey from the ancient origins of customer service to a vision of what it could become.

Part I: The Broken Promise revealed how the social contract of customer service was broken and why every interaction now feels like a betrayal of what was promised.

You've understood why customer service feels so personal even when the problems are obviously systemic. You've seen how companies profit from the gap between marketing promises and service delivery. You've learned why the customer service formula that worked for 4,000 years suddenly stopped working in the last few decades.

Part II: How We Got Here traced the history from personal accountability to systematized avoidance. You've seen how technology meant to serve customers became tools to avoid them.

You've discovered why the same innovations that should have made customer service better instead made it worse. You've understood how economic incentives shifted from rewarding customer satisfaction to punishing it. You've learned why "the customer is always right" went from business strategy to marketing slogan.

Part III: The System in Action exposed the economics behind bad service—the spreadsheet decisions that turn your frustration into corporate profit.

You've seen the actual calculations companies use to determine how much suffering is optimal. You've understood why technology is deployed to deflect rather than resolve. You've learned how industries that seem different all use the same playbook to avoid serving customers.

Part IV: The Way Forward provided the roadmap to fix customer service—specific, actionable strategies for customers, service professionals, and business leaders who want to build something better.

You've learned how to demand better service and actually get it. You've discovered how service professionals can drive change from within broken systems. You've seen how business leaders can turn customer service from a cost center into a competitive advantage.

Most importantly, you've understood that customer service can be fixed. The same mathematical precision that created this broken system can be used to build something better.

Hope, Not Despair

This book might have made you angry. It should. When you understand how deliberately customer service has been made terrible, anger is the appropriate response.

But this book wasn't just a diagnosis, it was a cure.

Customer service can be fixed. We've seen it work. We know what it takes. The tools exist. The knowledge exists. The technology exists.

What's been missing is the will to change and the understanding of why change is necessary.

Here's what gives us hope:

Customer power is growing: Social media, review platforms, and global connectivity mean that bad customer service can't be hidden the way it used to be. Companies that treat customers badly face immediate public consequences.

Worker power is growing: The labor shortage in customer service is forcing companies to treat their employees better, which inevitably leads to better customer treatment.

Technology is maturing: AI and automation are becoming sophisticated enough to actually help customers rather than just deflecting them. The same tools that have been used to avoid customers can be used to serve them better.

Economic pressure is building: The long-term costs of bad customer service are starting to show up in metrics that executives care about—customer acquisition costs, lifetime value, brand reputation, regulatory attention.

Generational change is coming: Leaders who grew up with terrible customer service are reaching positions where they can change it. They understand the costs because they've lived with them.

Competition is intensifying: In markets where products are becoming commoditized, customer experience is one of the few remaining differentiators. Companies that figure this out first will have massive advantages.

The Revolution Has Already Started

Some companies have already broken ranks with the industry consensus that customers should be avoided rather than served.

They're investing in human-centered service. They're using technology to enhance rather than replace human connection. They're measuring success by customer outcomes rather than internal efficiencies.

And they're winning. Not just in customer satisfaction scores, but in the metrics that matter to executives: growth, profitability, market share, and brand value.

The revolution in customer service won't come from regulations or consumer advocacy groups. It will come from companies that discover they can make more money by actually serving customers than by avoiding them.

Your Role in the Revolution

Whether you're a customer, a service professional, or a business leader, you have a role to play in fixing customer service.

As a customer, you have more power than you realize. You just need to know how to use it. This book has shown you how to demand better service and actually get it, how to reward companies that treat you well, and how to punish companies that don't.

As a service professional, you have the opportunity to drive change from within. You understand the problems better than anyone else. You see the gap between what customers need and what companies provide. This book has given you the tools and language to advocate for change in ways that executives will actually hear.

As a business leader, you have the power to break free from the industry consensus that customer service should be minimized rather than maximized. This book has shown you how to turn service from a cost center into a profit center, how to use customer satisfaction as a competitive weapon, and how to build systems that actually serve customers.

The Stakes Are Higher Than You Think

This isn't just about making customer service slightly less frustrating.

This is about whether we can build an economy that works for human beings or whether we'll accept an economy that systematically works against them.

This is about whether companies serve customers or whether customers serve companies.

This is about whether technology enhances human connection or replaces it entirely.

This is about whether the promise of capitalism—that competition will force companies to serve customers better—still works in the modern economy.

Customer service is the front line of the relationship between business and society. When that relationship breaks down, everything else becomes more difficult: trust in institutions, faith in markets, belief in progress itself.

The Path Forward

The story we've told you wasn't easy to hear. You've learned that most of your customer service frustrations aren't accidents but deliberate design choices. You've discovered that companies profit from your suffering in ways you probably never imagined.

But you've also learned that this system can be changed. That customer service can work. That companies can profit by serving customers rather than avoiding them.

The path forward requires understanding where we've been, how we got here, and why the current system persists despite making everyone miserable.

It requires acknowledging that the problem isn't technology or globalization or cultural change—it's incentives. And incentives can be changed.

Most importantly, it requires believing that we can do better. That customer service doesn't have to be universally terrible. That the relationship between companies and customers can be based on mutual respect rather than systematic contempt.

The Journey Continues

The social contract of customer service wasn't always broken. For most of human history, it worked because the incentives were aligned. Merchants who treated customers badly went out of business. Customers who were reasonable got good service.

To understand how we lost that alignment and how to get it back, we've gone back to the beginning. We've seen how customer service evolved from personal accountability to corporate avoidance, one broken promise at a time.

We've understood how a system that once worked for thousands of years became so thoroughly broken in just a few decades.

The story started with merchants who cared about their reputations and moved through corporations that profit from customer misery.

But it doesn't end there.

It ends with a new generation of companies and customers who refuse to accept that terrible service is inevitable. Who understand that the technology and knowledge exist to create something better. Who are willing to do the work to build it.

The revolution in customer service has already begun. The only question is whether you'll be part of it.

The choice and the responsibility is ours.

Customer service will improve exactly as much as we demand it improves and reward it for improving.

The accountability reset begins with you. Not tomorrow. Not when someone else goes first. Not when conditions are perfect.

Now.

Because we've learned that when customers can't leave, companies stop trying to keep them happy. When customers can vote with their wallets, companies compete for their satisfaction. When service professionals advocate for change, executives listen. When business leaders invest in service excellence, they gain competitive advantages.

The revolution in customer service doesn't start with companies or technology or regulations.

It starts with the recognition that we have the power to demand better, the knowledge to build better, and the responsibility to create the economy we want to live in.

The revolution begins now. The only question is whether you'll be part of it.

Visit WaitingForService.com and join the movement.

Because customer service doesn't have to be terrible.

It just has to change.

And change starts with you.

Amas Tenumah is a customer service industry veteran with 25 years of experience and author of Hold: The Suffering Economy of Customer Service And the Revolt That's Long Overdue. "Waiting for Service: An

Insider's Guide to Customer Service." He is a regular contributor to NPR, The Atlantic, NBC News, and other major media outlets. Contact him at amastenumah.com for speaking engagements and other services.

WORKS CITED

Aisera. "Omnichannel Customer Support." Aisera Blog, aisera.com/blog/omnichannel-customer-support/. Accessed 2024.

BBC Worklife. "Consumer Brands Leave Social Media." BBC, 12 July 2023, www.bbc.com/worklife/article/20230712-consumer-brands-leave-social-media-meta-threads.

BigCommerce. "Social Media Customer Service." BigCommerce Blog, www.bigcommerce.com/blog/social-media-customer-service/. Accessed 2024.

Brand24. "Social Media Customer Service for Brands." Brand24 Blog, brand24.com/blog/social-media-customer-service-for-brands/. Accessed 2024.

Business Dasher. "Social Media Customer Service Statistics." Business Dasher, www.businessdasher.com/social-media-customer-service-statistics/. Accessed 2024.

CMSWire. "X, Meta and the Great Social Media Meltdown." CMSWire, www.cmswire.com/digital-marketing/x-meta-and-the-great-social-media-meltdown/. Accessed 2024.

CustomerSure. "Social Media Customer Service." CustomerSure Blog, www.customersure.com/blog/social-media-customer-service/. Accessed 2024.

Flaunter. "Big Brands Are Leaving Social Media: Should You?" Flaunter Blog, www.flaunter.com/blog/big-brands-are-leaving-social-media-should-you. Accessed 2024.

Forbes Agency Council. "How to Use Social Media for Customer Service." Forbes, 23 Jan. 2024, www.forbes.com/councils/forbesagencycouncil/2024/01/23/how-to-use-social-media-for-customer-service/.

Fullview. "History of Customer Service." Fullview Blog, www.fullview.io/blog/history-of-customer-service. Accessed 2024.

---. "Social Media Is Changing Customer Service." Fullview Blog, www.fullview.io/blog/social-media-is-changing-customer-service. Accessed 2024.

GoCloud Group. "History of Customer Service: How Did It All Begin?" GoCloud Group, gocloud.group/history-of-customer-service-how-did-it-all-begin/. Accessed 2024.

Harvard Business Review. "Why Marketers Are Spending Less on Social Media." HBR, Oct. 2024, hbr.org/2024/10/why-marketers-are-spending-less-on-social-media?ab=HP-topics-image-10.

Hoory. "History of Customer Service: How Did It All Begin?" Hoory Blog, www.hoory.com/blog/i/history-of-customer-service-how-did-it-all-begin. Accessed 2024.

IBM Think. "Omnichannel Customer Service." IBM, www.ibm.com/think/topics/omnichannel-customer-service. Accessed 2024.

ICMI. "Is Your Social Media Customer Service Helping CX?" ICMI Resources, 2018, www.icmi.com/resources/2018/is-your-social-media-customer-service-helping-cx.

Knowledge@Wharton. "The Ignored Side of Social Media: Customer Service." Wharton School, University of Pennsylvania, knowledge.wharton.upenn.edu/article/ignored-side-social-media-customer-service/. Accessed 2024.

Landingi. "History of Social Media Marketing." Landingi, landingi.com/social-media-marketing/history/. Accessed 2024.

LinkedIn Business. "How Businesses Are Using Social Media for Customer Service." LinkedIn, www.linkedin.com/pulse/how-businesses-using-social-media-customer-service-3sixfive-bhkee. Accessed 2024.

LS Retail. "4 Omni-Channel Failures Easily Avoided with the Right Management System." LS Retail Resources, www.lsretail.com/resources/4-omni-channel-failures-easily-avoided-right-management-system. Accessed 2024.

---. "Omni-Channel Successes and Failures." *LS Retail Resources*, www.lsretail.com/resources/omni-channel-successes-and-failures. Accessed 2024.

Magenest. "Omnichannel Failure Examples." *Magenest*, magenest.com/en/omnichannel-failure-examples/. Accessed 2024.

McKinsey & Company. "Social Media as a Service Differentiator: How to Win." *McKinsey Capabilities*, www.mckinsey.com/capabilities/operations/our-insights/social-media-as-a-service-differentiator-how-to-win. Accessed 2024.

Nextiva. "Omnichannel Customer Service." *Nextiva Blog*, www.nextiva.com/blog/omnichannel-customer-service.html. Accessed 2024.

Ocoya. "Social Media Customer Support." *Ocoya Blog*, www.ocoya.com/blog/social-media-customer-support. Accessed 2024.

Our World in Data. "The Rise of Social Media." *Our World in Data*, ourworldindata.org/rise-of-social-media. Accessed 2024.

Payments Association. "The History of Social Media Marketing." *The Payments Association*, thepaymentsassociation.org/article/the-history-of-social-media-marketing/. Accessed 2024.

Qualtrics. "Experience Management: Social Media Customer Service." *Qualtrics*, www.qualtrics.com/experience-management/customer/social-media-customer-service/. Accessed 2024.

---. "Omnichannel Customer Service." *Qualtrics*, www.qualtrics.com/experience-management/customer/omnichannel-customer-service/. Accessed 2024.

Quirks. "Studies Chart the Evolution of Social Media as a Customer Service Channel." *Quirks*, www.quirks.com/articles/studies-chart-the-evolution-of-social-media-as-a-customer-service-channel. Accessed 2024.

Sana Commerce. "Reasons Your Omnichannel Strategy Is Failing." *Sana Commerce Blog*, www.sana-commerce.com/blog/reasons-your-omnichannel-strategy-is-failing/. Accessed 2024.

Sprinklr. "Omnichannel Customer Service." *Sprinklr CXM*, www.sprinklr.com/cxm/omnichannel-customer-service/. Accessed 2024.

Sprout Social. "Social Media Customer Service Statistics." *Sprout Social Insights*, sproutsocial.com/insights/social-media-customer-service-statistics/. Accessed 2024.

SquareTalk. "7 Benefits of Omnichannel Customer Service." *SquareTalk*, squaretalk.com/7-benefitsof-omnichannel-customer-service/. Accessed 2024.

TalkDesk. "How to Use Social Media as a Customer Service Channel." *TalkDesk Resources*, www.talkdesk.com/resources/infographics/how-to-use-social-media-as-a-customer-service-channel/. Accessed 2024.

TDMSBlog. "The Evolution of Social Media Customer Service." *TDMS Blog*, 5 Sept. 2024, tdmsblog.com/2024/09/05/the-evolution-of-social-media-customer-service/.

TeamSupport. "History of Customer Support Technology." *TeamSupport*, www.teamsupport.com/history-of-customer-support-technology/. Accessed 2024.

TechSee. "Omnichannel Customer Service: Challenges and Solutions." *TechSee Blog*, techsee.com/blog/omnichannel-customer-service-challenges-and-solutions/. Accessed 2024.

ThinkOwl. "Customer Service in the Age of Social Media." *ThinkOwl Blog*, www.thinkowl.com/blog/customer-service-in-the-age-of-social-media. Accessed 2024.

Zendesk. "Customer Service Through Social Media." *Zendesk Blog*, www.zendesk.com/blog/customer-service-through-social-media/. Accessed 2024.

---. "What Is Bad Customer Service?" *Zendesk Blog*, www.zendesk.com/blog/what-is-bad-customer-service/. Accessed 2024.

---. "What Omnichannel Really Means." *Zendesk Blog*, www.zendesk.com/blog/omnichannel-really-means/. Accessed 2024.

Zoom. "Omnichannel Customer Service." *Zoom Blog*, www.zoom.com/en/blog/omnichannel-customer-service/. Accessed 2024.

NOTES

Chapter 2: Historical Context

[1] Fullview, "History of Customer Service"; GoCloud Group, "History of Customer Service: How Did It All Begin?";

TeamSupport, "History of Customer Support Technology."

Chapter 4: Social Media and Customer Service

[2] Quirks, "Studies Chart the Evolution of Social Media as a Customer Service Channel."

[3] McKinsey & Company, "Social Media as a Service Differentiator: How to Win."

[4] Knowledge@Wharton, "The Ignored Side of Social Media: Customer Service."

[5] Sprout Social, "Social Media Customer Service Statistics."

Chapter 8: Technology and Omnichannel

[6] IBM Think, "Omnichannel Customer Service"; Zendesk, "What Omnichannel Really Means."

[7] Magenest, "Omnichannel Failure Examples"; LS Retail, "4 Omni-Channel Failures Easily Avoided with the Right Management System."

[8] TechSee, "Omnichannel Customer Service: Challenges and Solutions."

Acknowledgments

This book draws on twenty-five years of industry experience,

extensive client work, and comprehensive research into customer service

practices across industries. I am grateful to the researchers, journalists, and

industry analysts who have documented the evolution and systematic

challenges of customer service.

Special recognition goes to the research at McKinsey & Company,

Wharton School's Knowledge@Wharton, Harvard Business Review, IBM

Think, and Zendesk for their ongoing analysis of customer service trends

and failures. The customer service technology community, including

researchers at Sprout Social, Qualtrics, and various industry publications,

has provided valuable data and insights that inform this critique.

The customer service stories and examples throughout this book come

from publicly available sources, industry publications, and anonymized

professional experiences that respect confidentiality while illustrating

systematic industry patterns.

Additional thanks to the customer service professionals, frontline workers, and consumer advocates who continue to document and push for improvements in customer experience, often challenging conventional business practices that prioritize cost reduction over human dignity.

www.ingramcontent.com/pod-product-compliance
Lightning Source LLC
Chambersburg PA
CBHW030124240326
41458CB00121B/490